Lost Restaurants of Fredericksburg

MICHAEL BARR

Foreword by Mark Wieser

AMERICAN PALATE

Published by American Palate
A Division of The History Press
Charleston, SC
www.historypress.com

Front cover: *All images courtesy of Gillespie County Historical Society.*
Back cover, top: Rathskellar Bistro. *Author's photograph. Inset*: Pontotoc Weingarten. *Author's photograph.*

First published 2023

Manufactured in the United States

ISBN 9781467155113

Library of Congress Control Number: 2023938349

Notice: The information in this book is true and complete to the best of our knowledge. It is offered without guarantee on the part of the author or The History Press. The author and The History Press disclaim all liability in connection with the use of this book.

Contents

Opposite: Fischer and Wieser on Main, 315 East Main Street. *Author's photograph*.

Foreword

When I first began reading Mike Barr's takes on Fredericksburg food, I thought, *What makes this outsider think he is qualified to write about our food establishments?* Why, he didn't even grow up here! Moreover, he admitted that his food knowledge was not exactly comprehensive or sophisticated. Perhaps a fair assessment, but as I began to follow his weekly stories, I soon discovered he understood our take on food remarkably well, for an Ausländer!

I am not certain when we reached out to each other, but I treasure the fact that I can now call him a friend. He's grasped an understanding of places—those we both knew and know. Some, neither of us had known. Others are but faint memories. His writing makes us realize, sadly, that we treasure many far too lightly.

Mike did his homework diligently and accurately. He makes us aware that even as a small settlement nestled in the Texas Hill Country, we have quite a heritage, of which we should be very proud. How many of us ever thought that some places we once frequented would be so treasured? Many of the lost restaurants, their owners and their menus reveal who we were. No other could have accomplished that as well as Mike has in his *Lost Restaurants of Fredericksburg*.

Mark Wieser

Introduction

A Redneck in a Sushi Bar

The way you make an omelet reveals your character.
—Anthony Bourdain

A good deal of this book is devoted to German food, and I began writing it with two significant disadvantages. I am not German, and more to the point, I know very little about food. Like most people, I enjoy food (I often dream about it), but I rarely take the time to consider it beyond its most basic purpose.

I think about food when I'm hungry, but only in general terms. My food knowledge is, sadly, superficial. I know how to eat food (most of it, anyway) but very little about its often lengthy journey before it lands on my plate. In my world, food appears at the table ready to eat, not by magic but by a process I only understand in a distant sort of way.

The kitchen and I are but casual acquaintances. I am on speaking terms with the barbecue grill and the microwave, but otherwise, I can't cook a lick. Without my wife and the hospitality of friends, I'd starve or go broke eating out. I know my way around the dining room table like the back of my hand, but in the kitchen, five feet away, I am a stranger. I know the way to the refrigerator because there is beer in it.

And so, it is fair to ask, how could a bumpkin like me, with a knowledge gap (a canyon, really) wider than the Llano Estacado write a book about food? At first, I had no idea.

I was in a pickle, and there was no way to sugarcoat it. I had bitten off more than I could chew. I was out of my comfort zone—like a redneck in a sushi bar.

Finally, after a frustrating month of fits and starts, I took a leap of faith. I followed my nose, my intuition and my natural interests into uncharted culinary territory. As a result, the story that began to stew and simmer in my head was not so much about the flavor of food but more about the history and culture of food and drink in Fredericksburg, Texas—a territory I feel at least marginally qualified to write about.

Then, as I got a little more comfortable with the subject, a funny thing happened. I found my thoughts and feelings about food beginning to change (a mighty poor effort this would be if that were not the case). While I will never be a gourmet or call myself a foodie (not that I would ever want to), I pay a lot more attention to food these days—not only its smell, taste and texture but also where it came from and how it got here. Best of all, I discovered that food reflects the beliefs, the values, the customs and the love of the people who make it, and I find the cultural connections between food and people to be endlessly fascinating.

In the past, my food choices were often narrow and repetitive, but now I look for different food experiences. I am a more adventurous eater. I like to explore different restaurants. When I visit other countries, I want not just to see, hear, feel and smell the culture but taste it, as well. Even if the taste is not to my liking, I am better off for trying it. I learn from the experience. Growth requires risk.

Many thanks go out to the Küchenkaiserin (the empress of the kitchen) who saved me from starvation and to my friend Mark Wieser of Fischer and Wieser Specialty Foods of Fredericksburg. I showed Mark an early draft of this story. I would not have finished it without his encouragement.

Chapter 1

Call It Dinner

The people who give you their food give you their heart.
—Cesar Chavez

There's more to dining than a few moments of pleasure and a cigarette. Food is about relationships, rituals and symbolism. It all began the day a cave dweller accidently dropped the hindquarter of a wooly mammoth in the fire, shared it with his tribe and called it dinner. Chew on that for a minute.

Beyond taste and nutritional value, food connects us to our roots and reminds us of who we are. It is part of our culture and a direct connection to our history. It is a factor in our friendships, our religious practices, even our sex life.

Food is a link to our childhood. When an aroma from the kitchen triggers a pleasant memory from long ago, food becomes a magic carpet that transports us back to special times in our lives.

We relate to other people with food. It is a cultural expression of love and a symbol of family, fellowship, happiness, comfort and warmth. It is about sharing.

One of the most common ways of showing people we care about them is to have them over for dinner. Eating and drinking together become gestures of friendship and acts of peace and goodwill. Relationships are formed around food and differences put aside. Ancient enemies become allies when they eat and drink together.

Families in all cultures rely heavily on food in their daily routines. Plans are made and problems are solved around the household hub and home communications center, a.k.a. the dining room table. Preparing and consuming food together is one way the adult members of a family pass on the culture to the younger generation.

Food can be a symbol of social standing. In Russia, only the elite can afford caviar. In ancient Greece, ambrosia was food for the gods.

Food and drink have always been closely connected to religion. Christian churches use bread and wine in the practice of Holy Communion. Muslims fast during Ramadan. Some Jews follow a strict Kosher diet. Buddhists and Hindus are vegetarians.

Even the composition and preparation of food can be religiously symbolic. Traditional baklava, a Middle Eastern pastry and an ancestor to German strudel, has thirty-three layers—one layer for each year of the life of Jesus. St. Agatha's Breasts are round buns, resembling bosoms, that honor St. Agatha, who was martyred after having her breasts cut off for refusing the advances of a Roman magistrate. Michaelmas Bannock (St. Michael's Bannock) is a Gaelic bread made of rye, oats and barley without using metal instruments and served on the eve of the Feast of St. Michael the Archangel.

Throughout history, different cultures have credited certain foods with the power to do a lot more than fill the stomach. The ancient world believed garlic had healing powers and provided protection against the plague. Egyptian pharaohs fed garlic to their slaves to increase their strength and stamina. In Slavic countries, garlic keeps vampires, and everyone else, at a distance.

Aphrodisiacs, named for Aphrodite, the Greek goddess of love, form the connection between food and sex. The ancient Greeks believed figs boosted sexual potency. The most famous aphrodisiac, the oyster, dates to the Romans, who were known to shuck a few before orgies.

In some cultures, eating black-eyed peas on New Year's Day brings twelve months of good fortune. Residents of the American South eat Hoppin' John, a slave dish of black-eyed peas, ham and rice, to improve their chances of good luck. Citizens of Germany, Poland and the Czech Republic eat pickled herring at the stroke of midnight on January 1 for a prosperous New Year.

From the beginning, food has been a big part of celebrations, both religious and secular. Many European cultures have a fall festival, including food, drink and music, to celebrate the end of the harvest season. There is a feast to celebrate the Chinese New Year. Mardi Gras (Fat Tuesday) represents the last wild night of eating rich, fatty foods before Lent (for Christians, a period of fasting in preparation for Easter).

The Thanksgiving holiday is loaded with food symbolism. After the Civil War, the United States government encouraged the Thanksgiving feast as a way to heal the country. Even the foods for the Thanksgiving meal (turkey and pumpkin pie) represent America.

Food is an expression of cultural identity. When immigrants take up residence in a new country, they bring the food of their homeland with them. Their food is a symbol of pride and a way of preserving their culture.

Food, however, does not remain exactly the same, especially in new surroundings. Ingredients change when traditional ones are no longer available. Preparation techniques change. Ethnic restaurants sometimes alter food to give it wider appeal. Foods of different cultures fuse to take food in an entirely new and exciting direction.

Food changes, even people change, but what doesn't change is the way food reflects a culture's history and values. Because Chinese society places a premium on harmony, their food is carefully balanced (sweet and sour,

Rathskeller Bistro, 260 East Main Street. *Author's photograph.*

Hondo's on Main, 312 West Main Street. *Author's photograph.*

for example). Mexican food, like the people, is a spicy, festive blend of Spanish, Native American, Caribbean and African cultures. American fast food reflects a culture that is always in a hurry. The German people are orderly, literal and direct, and so is the food. German food doesn't have fancy names. What you see is what you get. The food tastes exactly the way it sounds.

In the 1840s, a group of German immigrants came to Fredericksburg in the Texas Hill Country. Their culture helped them survive on the frontier, where the necessities of life did not come easy.

But that culture has a complicated history. The United States fought two wars with Germany in the twentieth century. Although the Hill Country Germans had proven their patriotism and loyalty to America over and over again, their culture made them suspect. To a sizeable part of the country, Germans were the enemy, wherever they lived. As a result, German culture, including the food, found little respect in mainstream America.

Fortunately, the postwar American generation put those feelings aside, and the German culture got its swagger back. Today, visitors fill the streets of Fredericksburg to experience the culture many Americans once dismissed.

Tubby's Ice House, 318 East Austin Street. *Author's photograph.*

The beauty of the Texas Hill Country and the allure of the German culture draw visitors and residents to Fredericksburg from all over the world. The result is that this once solidly German colony is now a modern global community and a popular tourist destination.

Fredericksburg honors its rich German heritage but celebrates its diverse population. The changing menus of the cafés and restaurants along Fredericksburg's busy Main Street reflect that cultural shift.

Chapter 2

Just Deserts

There is a friendly tie of some sort between music and eating.
—Thomas Hardy

Because Fredericksburg, Texas, is a German town, the native food around here has never gotten its just deserts. Authentic German food, after all, seems out of place in modern food culture. It has a reputation for being starchy, heavy and filling—the kind of food that sticks to your ribs and stays there.

German food is not chic, trendy or sexy. It is rarely highlighted on the Food Channel. It is blue collar and unpretentious. I have always thought that the reason German food is so lightly regarded is that it's a little too close to home cooking for most of us to appreciate the nuances. It's not fancy enough. Schnitzel, after all, looks a lot like chicken fried steak.

No doubt about it, German food suffers from an image problem, often self-inflicted. Blutwurst (blood sausage) and Leberwurst (liver sausage) never had a chance. The names sound unappealing in English—even worse in German. Schwartenmagen sounds innocent enough (and the taste is not bad), until the person eating it discovers he is munching on food scraps cooked in a pig's stomach.

Authentic German food, like the German people themselves, is not subtle. Unlike the French and Italians, whose food names often sound intriguing, even erotic, German food is honest, sensible and straightforward. It is what it is. No fluff. And eating it is an adventure—not always a predictable one, but an adventure nonetheless.

The first lesson to learn about traditional Fredericksburg food is that the old Hill Country Germans, from the first settlers to the World War II generation, valued food not always for its flavor but as a matter of survival. Food didn't come easy. For much of their history, going back to the old country, the Germans had to work hard to get food and just as hard to prepare it. Then they had to dry it, salt it, pickle it or can it to make it last through the winter.

Because food was scarce, the Hill Country Germans learned to use every part of the cow, pig, deer, onion and cabbage, even parts not normally on the menu. Creative cooks found ways to use ears, skin, feet, tongue and brains. Nothing went to waste.

Those things aside, I have found that authentic German food, well prepared and served in the proper atmosphere, is both interesting and delicious. Kochkäse (German cooked cheese) and chips or crackers make a great appetizer. Spaetzle, a doughy German noodle, tastes especially good after the first chill in October.

While some German dishes really are heavy on the sausage and potatoes, there are also wonderful earthy breads (German bakeries are fabulous), creamy cheeses, rich stews, crispy brined vegetables, soft noodles and delicate

The Biergarten at Altdorf Restaurant, 310 West Main Street. *Author's photograph.*

dumplings, accompanied by brawny beers and lusty wines and finished with fruity cakes, pies and strudel.

But the most important characteristic of German food is that it is meant to be prepared and eaten with others. Half the fun of stuffing deer sausage is stuffing it with family and friends—and having a few beers while you're doing it. I've watched mothers, daughters and granddaughters in the kitchen, making Gefüllte Nudeln (filled noodles), laughing and talking in two languages, flour flying through the air like smoke. As my favorite Hausfrau always says, "German food is made with love."

For Germans, food is about much more than taste. German food is a social experience. Eating and drinking are communal activities. (That's why Germans love beer gardens.) Being able to talk and eat at the same time is a definite advantage. And keep the napkins handy.

In Germany, and later in the Hill Country of Texas, the Germans had a hard existence. They spent much of the year laying in food and resources for the winter. Then, in the fall, after harvest, the whole community came together for an Erntefest (harvest festival) with music, dancing, beer and food.

Fall festivals are still a tradition in the Texas Hill Country. Those Germans know how to throw a party.

Above all, German food is about celebrating life. It is loud and festive. It pairs nicely with beer, music, dancing, laughter and conversation. It is about eating and drinking in cheerful, noisy company—better enjoyed in a rowdy beer garden than in a quiet, polite restaurant. Once you understand the communal nature of German food, you get a glimpse of what it means to be German.

Chapter 3

Like a Visit to Saxony

Gute Nahrung und Ruhepause *(good food and rest).*
—Dr. Wilhelm Keidel's formula for a happy, healthy life

Fredericksburg, Texas, is the closest thing to Germany this side of Düsseldorf. In fact, German was a strong second language in this part of the Hill Country until a generation ago.

Immigrants from the German states settled Fredericksburg in 1846. The leader of the settlement, Baron Otfried Hans Freiherr von Meusebach, chose a townsite in the rolling Hill Country, sixty miles northwest of New Braunfels, in an isolated valley where two streams joined a few miles above the Pedernales River.

Meusebach named the settlement Fredericksburg (Friedrichsburg) after Prince Friedrich of Prussia, a friend and member of the Adelsverein (Noblemen's Association), the immigration society that sponsored the German immigrants and helped them settle in Texas.

Surveyor Hermann Willke laid out the town, not around a Spanish-style town square but like a German village along the Rhine, with one wide Hauptstraße (Main Street) running between the two creeks. The unassuming settlers named one of the creeks Town Creek and the other Baron's Creek, after Baron von Meusebach.

Main Street runs straight as a gun barrel through Fredericksburg, southeast to northwest. It is about ninety feet wide. Legend says that Hermann Willke made Main Street (commonly called San Saba Street until the twentieth

A cozy Fredericksburg Sunday House. *Author's photograph.*

century) wide enough to allow a wagon pulled by a team of horses to do an easy U-turn in the middle of the block.

The original village measured thirteen blocks long and six blocks wide. As time passed, more settlers arrived, and the town slowly took shape. Soon, a number of cabins had gone up between Hauptstraße and Baron's Creek, along what are now San Antonio, Creek, Peach and Ufer Streets.

The Adelsverein gave each Fredericksburg family a town lot and a parcel of land out in the countryside. Many of the settlers lived on their farms in the country but built tiny Sunday Houses on their town lots for use on weekends and holidays. A number of those historic Sundays Houses still stand.

The Germans who came to the Texas Hill Country left behind a homeland teeming with social chaos, economic hardship and political discontent to take part in a remarkable experiment—a colony of free men, women and children, determined to build a new and better life for themselves from the ground up, in the wilds of Southwest Texas, miles beyond the frontier line.

Compared to other frontiersmen, the German settlers had an advantage that allowed them to survive the lean years. Unlike the rugged individualists who typically moved west with the frontier, the Germans had a communal spirit and a culture of working together for the good of the whole. After a difficult start, Fredericksburg took root, leaving a strong Germanic stamp on the Texas Hill Country that endures to this day.

An old Indian path called the Pinta Trail crossed this part of the Hill Country. In the eighteenth century, the trail became the primary route from San Antonio to the Mission San Luis de las Amarillas on the San Saba River (near present-day Menard). Travelers in both directions along the Pinta Trail made the area around Fredericksburg a crossroads and a meeting ground for Native American, Spanish, Mexican, southern Anglo, German, northern European and African cultures.

Spanish priests planted crosses on tops of hills to mark the Pinta Trail. Cross Mountain (Kreuzberg) on the northern edge of Fredericksburg is named for a wooden Spanish cross found on its summit. The cross dated to a century before the founding of the town. It had fallen down but lay where it fell.

In the beginning, Fredericksburg's very existence hinged on a remarkable relationship between Baron von Meusebach and the Comanche. Meusebach impressed the natives with his bravery, his honesty, his altitude (he stood six feet, two inches) and his flaming red hair and beard (the Comanches called him El Sol Colorado—the Red Sun—in Spanish).

With Meusebach's guidance, the Germans and the Comanche got along remarkably well. Their 1847 peace treaty cracked but never broke. The Natives danced in the streets when the Germans laid the cornerstone for the Vereins Kirche (community church) in 1847. Chief Santana brought one of his wives to Fredericksburg to give birth.

In those first delicate years, with the survival of the colony hanging in the balance, the Fredericksburg Germans had a closer bond with the Natives than with their distant Anglo neighbors. Frederick Law Olmsted, the writer and landscape architect who designed Central Park in New York City, traveled to Fredericksburg in the 1850s. He wrote, "After the foundation of Fredericksburg by the German settlers, the principal supplies of food were obtained from the Indians, and the people were almost in consternation when the forts were first established near, and the Indians withdrew their supplies and their profitable barter."

Cross Mountain. A sentinel over the city. *Author's photograph.*

In 1848, not long after the state formed Gillespie County and named Fredericksburg the county seat, the U.S. Army established Fort Martin Scott on the banks of Barons Creek just outside Fredericksburg. The fort, built to protect settlers from hostile Natives, closed in 1853 (the frontier line had moved west).

More than the Natives, even more than the wild frontier environment, the Confederates posed the greatest threat to the developing German colony. The Civil War stretched the bonds of the community to its limits.

Officer's quarters, Fort Martin Scott, Fredericksburg. *Author's photograph.*

Most Germans were Unionists and opposed to slavery, and they suffered considerably for it. After Confederates massacred a group of German Unionists on the Nueces River in 1862, the Confederacy placed Fredericksburg and all of Gillespie County under martial law for the duration of the war.

The Germans responded to the turmoil by keeping to themselves. They maintained their independence and stayed out of state and national affairs as much as possible.

As a result, Fredericksburg remained an isolated German village, with a European culture and traditions markedly different from the other parts of Texas. German remained the dominant language until World War II. (The *Wochenblatt*, the German language newspaper, continued in print until the mid-twentieth century.) The town had a European flavor in architecture, language, food and folkways. Because of its location, far from outside influences, Fredericksburg held to those customs for generations.

The isolation produced a society that was remarkably self-sufficient. Citizens produced most of their own foods. They brewed their own beer and made their own wine. They grew and cured their own tobacco. Teamsters hauled in those necessities not produced locally.

Although isolated from the rest of the world, the Germans of Fredericksburg made a good life for themselves. The people here enjoyed a standard of living unknown elsewhere on the Texas frontier.

The Germans had a flair for organizing, and they used it to create their own amusements. They held shooting contests (Schützenfests) and singing competitions (Sängerfests). Citizens made their own music and produced their own plays in the German language. Beginning in the early twentieth century, they loved to watch the Fredericksburg Giants play baseball, and they followed the team to Kerrville, Mason, Comfort, Llano, Stonewall, Hye and Albert.

The Germans enjoyed food, beer, laughter and conversation with family and good friends. They had fun. They celebrated the German way of life.

There is an untranslatable German word used to describe the warm feeling of sharing food and spirits with family and friends. The word is Gemütlichkeit, and it goes to the heart of what it means to be German.

The Germans made a home in Texas, but to an Ausländer (outsider), Gillespie County felt like a foreign country. On a trip to Fredericksburg in 1907, Ellen Maury Slayden, wife of San Antonio congressman James Luther Slayden, wrote, "It [Fredericksburg] was so old worldly, it was like a visit to Saxony."

German was the dominant language. People in Fredericksburg called the few citizens who couldn't speak German "Amerikaners"—and not always in a complimentary way.

Non–German speakers who came here to stay quickly learned German out of necessity. *Fredericksburg Standard* editor Art Kowert recalled moving to Fredericksburg as a child.

"I couldn't speak a word of German," he wrote. "At the time (1914–15) it was either learn to speak German or have no playmates. We learned German pretty quick."

The railroad came to town in 1913, bringing hope that the train would be a quick and easy connection to the outside world. But this train was surprisingly slow and uncertain. Frequent accidents and derailments interrupted service for days at a time.

Travel by automobile wasn't any better. Gillespie County had little pavement and few bridges. Cars had to ford creeks and rivers. A seventy-mile trip by automobile from Fredericksburg to San Antonio or Austin, the nearest towns of any size, turned into an all-day trip—one way.

The narrow roads meandered up and down the sides of hills. Model Ts, not equipped with fuel pumps, had to back up the steepest inclines in reverse to keep gasoline flowing from the rear fuel tanks to the carburetors.

The difficulties of getting in and out made Fredericksburg off-limits to all but the most determined travelers. As late as 1930 close to 90 percent of Gillespie County residents were descendants of the original settlers.

In the early twentieth century, Germans comprised the largest non-English-speaking immigrant group in America. Many American cities had German-language newspapers, schools and clubs. Catholic and Lutheran churches operated schools that taught the German language and culture to the younger generation. At the time, no one thought too much about it.

Then World War I began, and a wave of anti-German hysteria swept the country. Many non-Germans doubted that American and German cultures could mix. German Americans felt threatened. Violence broke out in some places. German pride suffered. Some Hill Country Germans toned down their German-ness as a show of patriotism and as a way to get along.

Close observers could see a slow erosion of the German culture. In 1923, Fredericksburg historian Julia Estill wrote that the older generation longs for "the times of real Deutsch Gemütlichkeit, which they feel will never return."

"The days of Skat [a German card game] and pinochle are over," she continued. "Beer suppe, Hasenpfeffer [rabbit stew] and Wienerschnitzel are delicacies of the past." The young people "no longer talk proudly of 'Der alt Kaiser Wilhelm' and 'unser Vaterland' in the pure German language of their forefathers."

While proud of their heritage, the Hill Country Germans were Americans first. They proved it during World War I. Fifteen Gillespie County men died in the war, including Lieutenant Louis Jordan of Fredericksburg, the first Texas officer killed in action.

As late as 1940, Fredericksburg remained an ethnic outpost with limited contact with the outside world. To some visitors in the 1930s and '40s, Fredericksburg had the feel of a German village along the Rhine, stuck in the nineteenth century.

On the eve of World War II, many people in Fredericksburg spoke functional English, but the language of home, church and street was Stadt Krick Deutsch (Town Creek German), a blend of several German dialects brought to Texas by the pioneers, with new words absorbed or made up to fit the situation.

For example, no German word existed for "skunk" (Stinkkatze) or "armadillo" (Panzerschwein—armored pig). Even the word "Krick" does not exist in German. It obviously comes from the word "creek." Locals made it up.

Today, there are only a few thousand people left on earth who speak what some experts call Texas German. Almost all of the speakers are senior citizens in New Braunfels, Seguin and the Texas Hill Country. Linguists predict that the dialect will be dead by 2040.

Modern Texas embraces the culture of the German Hill Country, but the opposite was true between 1915 and 1970. Much of Texas distrusted the German-speaking communities.

A state law passed in the aftermath of World War I mandated English-only instruction in Texas schools. Consequently, Hill Country students spoke two languages. They spoke English in the classroom but German on the playground.

In 1940, Colonel Alfred Petsch of Fredericksburg wrote in the *Fredericksburg Standard*,

> *For at least thirty years, we have observed an ever latent and sometimes affirmative prejudice against American citizens of German descent. This prejudice appears to be general throughout the state, throughout the entire South. Regrettable as it is, there apparently is no escape from it; though manifestly unjust and painfully embarrassing, it must be tolerated as there is little to be done about it.*

In some parts of the country, ridiculing Germans, including German-Americans, was acceptable—almost fashionable. Some Texas towns outside the German belt banned German classical music. Frankfurters became hot dogs. Sauerkraut became victory cabbage. Hamburgers became victory steaks. I have heard from more than one source that government agents regularly came to Fredericksburg during World War II to read the German language newspaper (the *Wochenblatt*) to be sure it contained no secret coded messages to the Nazis.

World War II proved those concerns groundless. At least forty-two Gillespie County men died in the war. Admiral Chester Nimitz, a German-American born in Fredericksburg, commanded the Pacific Fleet. When the chips were down, Fredericksburg and Gillespie County proved to be as patriotic as any community in America. More than most.

Still, the anti-German feelings that prevailed for much of the twentieth century took a toll on the German Hill Country. The rich German culture lost some of its energy. It rebounded somewhat after 1945, but it was never as distinct as it was before.

The erosion of the culture accelerated after World War II, when paved roads and concrete bridges made travel in and out of Fredericksburg easier and faster. Visitors came to Gillespie County to see Enchanted Rock, Balanced Rock and other natural wonders. Fredericksburg families traveled outside the Hill Country, many for the first time. The German Hill Country opened up. Outside influences softened the most distinctive characteristics of the German culture.

Other forces dismantled cultural barriers and altered society in ways no one could have imagined in the years before the powerful new technologies of the twentieth century.

On May 5, 1933, someone inside the Leo J. Blanchard Sporting Goods Store in Fredericksburg (located in the old Dietz Bakery building) threw a switch. I've probably watched too many Frankenstein movies, but I like to think that the lights dimmed and sparks flew. Witnesses noticed a humming sound, followed by the smell of something burning. Seconds later, Fredericksburg's first radio station, call letters WTTH, was on the air.

In the 1930s, radio entered its golden age. Stations, like WOAI in San Antonio, popped up all over the country. At the same time, radio sets became smaller and more affordable.

Radio was the gin and tonic that helped many Americans forget their economic troubles. Radio brought music and laughter and lessened the feeling of isolation in rural communities like Fredericksburg.

People who had never been out of Gillespie County could, with a radio and a little imagination, have box seats at Wrigley Field or be front row center at Radio City Music Hall.

Automobiles and radios opened the door to the outside world. As a result, the postwar generation of Fredericksburg young people came of age with a stronger connection to the outside world than with the local culture. They looked out more than in. They grew up under the influence of television, perhaps the greatest social force in the twentieth century. Television spread a mass culture that made America a more homogeneous society.

In the 1950s, Fredericksburg teens drove cars, went to the drive in, ate fast food, watched *American Bandstand* and bought Elvis records—just like teens in New York, Los Angeles, Dallas and Houston. German was still spoken in Fredericksburg, but fewer young people spoke it fluently. Fredericksburg was beginning to look, and sound, like any other small town in America.

Then, in 1960, Lyndon Johnson from nearby Stonewall became vice president of the United States. Three years later, after the assassination of President Kennedy, LBJ moved into the White House.

Suddenly, the eyes of the world focused on the president's home in Gillespie County. Government workers, journalists and tourists from all over the world invaded Stonewall, once a sleepy village known for its peach orchards and its button factory.

The big problem was that Stonewall had barely enough motel space for a small family reunion. When dignitaries stayed overnight at the LBJ Ranch, Lady Bird sometimes asked her neighbors to help with the overflow.

When the president came home to the LBJ Ranch in Stonewall, many in the press corps stayed thirteen miles away in Fredericksburg, and it wasn't long before reporters discovered the old-world charm of the place. They wrote stories about the German culture—which, with their help, was slowly disappearing—and introduced Fredericksburg to the rest of the world.

Walter Cronkite, the most famous newsman in America, made several trips to the Texas Hill Country in the 1960s. He stayed at the Sunday House Motel in Fredericksburg. When he wasn't with President Johnson, Cronkite played tennis at Lady Bird Johnson Park or had dinner at one of the restaurants in town.

Luckenbach Store and Post Office, Luckenbach, Texas. *Author's photograph.*

Soon, the world saw the culture of the Hill Country Germans in a whole new light. The old anti-German feelings began to fade. Visitors came to Fredericksburg—in droves.

Texans outside the Hill Country gained a new appreciation for German culture. In 1969, the State Fair of Texas held a German Day, with music, folk dancing, singing, food and drink under a large tent. The Beethoven Brass Band of San Antonio performed a special concert. After decades of living in the shadows, German pride came out into the sunlight.

Then, in the 1970s, America discovered the inspired craziness at Luckenbach—a suburb of Fredericksburg, you might say—focusing even more attention on the Hill Country. The number of tourists following Willie, Waylon and Jerry Jeff to the Luckenbach World's Fair, the Hell Hath No Fury Like a Woman Scorned Chili Cook Off and the Mud Dauber Festival reached levels no one had ever dreamed of.

Fredericksburg slowly gained a reputation as an exotic locale and a tourist attraction. In 1976, Austin TV personality Cactus Pryor wrote,

> *You can visit another country just 1½ hours from Austin. We did last Saturday. A delightful land of foreign accents, ancient rocks, tin and wooden buildings, home-baked breads and other delightfully different foods. A land of unbelievably wide avenues and shady streets still swept by the natives. There is a stately cathedral with stained-glass windows and paintings that would move a Rembrandt. We listened to folk songs sung in a foreign tongue and heard natives speaking in a still different language. We tasted wine made by our host with grapes from his own vineyard. And we didn't even need a passport because anyone can go to Fredericksburg, Texas.*

By the 1980s, Fredericksburg had been discovered. The town had thirty-eight restaurants, thirteen motels, three art galleries and twenty antique stores. Business along Main Street picked up.

And Hill Country life was contagious. People began moving to Fredericksburg, both into town and to some of the exclusive subdivisions out in the countryside. The price of real estate skyrocketed.

Today, wineries outnumber peach stands along Highway 290, between Fredericksburg and Johnson City. Fredericksburg is the point of departure for tours to the over one hundred wineries and tasting rooms in the Hill Country.

Log house, Fredericksburg. *Author's photograph.*

In 2022, visitors spent over $100 million to eat, drink, sleep and shop in Fredericksburg and Gillespie County. Tourism long ago surpassed agriculture as the driver of the local economy.

But progress comes with a price. As soon as the world discovered Fredericksburg, the town's German culture began eroding faster than ever. With each passing generation, Fredericksburg's authenticity as a German community diminishes.

The tradeoff is that few small towns in the world have as much energy as Fredericksburg. With a population of eleven thousand, modern Fredericksburg has over three hundred B&Bs, guest houses and inns and twenty hotels, not to mention some of the best restaurants, world-class museums, art galleries, wine gardens, drinking establishments and sunsets in the country. The community theater is going strong in Fredericksburg, and there is a flourishing live music scene.

Each year, thousands of visitors from around the world come to Fredericksburg for Oktoberfest, Night in Old Fredericksburg, the Gillespie County Fair (the oldest county fair in Texas), the Fourth of July Parade (the

Messina Hof Winery, Fredericksburg. *Author's photograph.*

best small town parade there is), the horse races and many other festivals throughout the year. In 2017, *Southern Living* magazine named Fredericksburg the best small town in Texas.

The evolution of Fredericksburg, from an isolated German settlement to a popular twenty-first century food and drink destination, got its shaky start 176 years ago. That the early settlers didn't starve to death is a tribute to their determination and the survival skills they brought with them from Germany to the wild Texas frontier.

Chapter 4

Everything but the Squeal

In wine there is wisdom, in beer there is strength, in water there is bacteria.
—David Auerbach

Toward evening on May 8, 1846, after sixteen days of hard travel from New Braunfels, the first German settlers to arrive in the Texas Hill Country pitched camp under a canopy of post oak trees along the banks of a small creek. Their first meal consisted of bear meat, roasted to a golden brown over a roaring fire. In his book *Fredericksburg, Texas—The First Fifty Years*, Robert Penniger wrote, "Mrs. Friedrich Lochte [Dorothea], the mother of Fritz Lochte, to the enjoyment and delight of the company, ate the head of the bear, which she said was very tasty."

In a light-hearted way, that story illustrates a serious fact of life in the early days of Fredericksburg. Food didn't exactly grow on trees.

The early settlers were constantly on the hunt for their next meal. They lived off the land. They took what the countryside offered and made the most of it. They never took food for granted.

Those first settlers woke up the next morning and immediately went to work raising tents and arbor shelters. Then the eight immigration society soldiers, about twenty wagon drivers and several capable young men mounted up and returned to New Braunfels, leaving the men, women and children to face the wilderness as best they could.

Food became an immediate concern as well as a subject of long-range planning for the settlers. Early on, they fenced a plot of ground for cultivation of a society garden and built a log warehouse to store provisions.

The scarcity of food taught Hill Country cooks to be resourceful. For example, when families butchered hogs, they used not just the ham, loin and shoulder but also the Rinde (skin), ears and feet—"everything but the squeal." Cows produced not only steaks but livers, hearts, stomachs, tongues and brains. Nothing went to waste. That rule guided Hill Country cooks for generations.

Fortunately, the original settlers in Fredericksburg brought food traditions and preparation techniques with them that fit their new situation on the Texas frontier. It turns out the Germans had a long history of making everything count when it came to food.

There was a time long ago when the German states of Europe were relatively isolated, especially compared to Mediterranean countries to the south. While trading ships from foreign lands introduced Spain, France, Italy and Greece to exotic foods, drinks and spices from around the world, Germans, by necessity, ate local.

Of course, German food had regional variations. Seafood is a staple in northern cities. The western regions have been influenced by French cuisine. Eastern Germany, a poorer region, grows a lot of starchy grains and potatoes. Bavaria is known for sausages.

That being said, Germany lies roughly along the same latitude as Newfoundland. The relatively cold weather and short growing season over much of the country produced a particular diet, rich in grains, dairy and meat.

Hearty grains like wheat, barley, rye and hops grew well in much of Germany. Consequently, the Germans ate a lot of Brot (bread), both the lighter wheat bread and the heavier rye and pumpernickel, at Frühstück (breakfast), Mittagessen (lunch—the main meal of the day) and Abengessen (dinner—a smaller evening meal, usually served cold, consisting of bread, dry sausage, cheese and some kind of vegetable).

Sheep, cows and goats thrived on the grassy German steppes. Milk, butter and cheese became important foods in the German diet.

The long German winter emphasized old-world food-preserving techniques such as pickling, salting, smoking and curing, and those culinary skills came in handy when the immigrants came to Texas. The German families in the Hill Country still use those ancient preserving methods to make dry sausage, jerky, Sauerbraten (pickled roast), Salzgurken (salted cucumbers) and Sauerkraut (pickled cabbage).

Any discussion of German cuisine without including beer would be a significant slipup. Germans love beer, with food and without. When they discovered it is anyone's guess, but it was love at first sight. Beer is a big part of the German culture.

The Babylonians and the Egyptians probably developed the art of brewing beer about 10,000 BC. Beer may have been the first man-made drink. The Babylonians and the Egyptians passed the art of brewing on to the Romans, who brought it to Germany. The Romans considered beer a Barbarian drink and the perfect beverage for the vulgar Teutons.

Until the twentieth century, health-conscious Europeans of all ages preferred beer and wine over water, which was often contaminated and unsafe to drink.

Beer has a close association with the early church. German monks started brewing beer in the Middle Ages. They liked their beer anytime, but they had a special fondness for it during Lent.

The monks weren't allowed food during Lent, but they could drink all the beer they wanted. They considered beer liquid bread. Drinking beer kept the faith. Monks called their beer "Sankt Vater"—Holy Father beer.

In Germany, brewing beer for public consumption is governed by the Reinheitsgebot (German Beer Purity Law) passed in 1613. The law keeps German beer pure, natural and free from unhealthy and cheap ingredients. The law is still in effect today.

All the beer and starchy foods gave German cuisine a reputation for being heavy and filling but not particularly flavorful. It was hearty food for people who worked the fields.

The German diet did expand over time. The Romans introduced fruit orchards and vineyards to Germany. Then Cologne became a trading center and acted as a gateway to culinary influences from Poland, Hungary, Turkey, Russia and China.

Some of the food many people think is German actually came from other countries. Sauerkraut, a pickled fermented cabbage, originally came from China, where cabbage fermented in rice wine. The men who built the Great Wall ate a lot of pickled cabbage. Some evidence suggests Sauerkraut came to Europe with Ghengis Kahn.

Schnitzel, known the world over as a German delicacy, can actually be traced to the Byzantine Empire, brought to Germany by the Arabs. Schnitzel is a tender, boneless piece of meat that is breaded, fried and served with a wedge of lemon. Wienerschnitzel is made from veal. Jägerschnitzel (hunter's schnitzel) comes with a mushroom sauce.

The Germans who settled the Texas Hill Country brought these food traditions from Germany. Because the Hill Country was so isolated, these traditions stayed remarkably pure and intact through the generations. The food and preservation techniques of the Hill Country Germans changed little from the settlement of Fredericksburg until the end of World War II.

Chapter 5
An Acquired Taste

I've long believed that good food, good eating, is all about risk.
—Anthony Bourdain

Hill Country cooks worked miracles in the kitchen. Using food skills and recipes they learned from their mothers and grandmothers, they fed their families in the face of short food supplies, inadequate storage methods and small household budgets.

Madeleine Oestreich grew up in Fredericksburg in the 1930s. Her childhood food experiences reflected the foods and preparation techniques the settlers brought from Germany almost a hundred years earlier.

> *Most of our food depended on what was available and what was in season. We had a garden at our house in town where we grew fresh vegetables. Some of our neighbors had milk cows. We didn't have a cow, but the milkman delivered milk twice a week. He left the milk on the front porch of our house on South Mesquite Street.*
>
> *Breakfast was usually homemade bread and cereal. We had chickens, so we sometimes had eggs.*
>
> *Some mornings my mother would beat a couple of eggs in a bowl, pour in some milk and season it with salt and pepper. She would soak day-old bread in the mixture, and then brown both sides of the bread in a skillet.*
>
> *She called it Eierbrodt (egg bread). Today we call it French toast. Same thing.*

Occasionally my mother made brains and eggs. She usually bought the brains from Henke's Meat Market.

Lunch was the main meal of the day. My father was the city clerk, and he always came home for lunch.

Meat was expensive during the Depression, so we only had it twice a week—at lunch on Wednesdays and at lunch on Sundays. Wednesday lunches were special because we had meat from the meat market—usually Henke's Meat Market on Main Street across from the Nimitz Hotel (today the Outpost at Luckenbach on Main). We usually had beef. Sometimes it was ground meat or sometimes veal. Occasionally we had beef tongue. We also had liver and heart or heart and dumplings. For Sunday lunch we had baked chicken. The main course was a hen that had stopped laying eggs.

For lunch the rest of the week we had vegetables, fresh from the garden or canned if it was wintertime. There wasn't always a variety of food, but my mother did her best. She would say in German, "Tonight we're having potatoes, cabbage and beans." The next night she would change it up and say, "Tonight we're having cabbage, beans and potatoes." Same vegetables, just in a different order. It was her little joke.

We had beans for lunch every Monday because Monday was wash day. My mother spent all day washing our clothes. There wasn't time to do much else. She would slow cook beans in a pot while she did the washing.

We ate a lot of potatoes from the garden, but mother prepared them in different ways. One night we had fried potatoes, one night creamed potatoes and one night mashed potatoes.

If the corn was in season, we had roasting ears (corn on the cob) for lunch. There were six of us if we were all there, and we had two ears each. Twelve ears of corn made a meal.

Of course, we always had bread and butter. My mother baked bread every day or so.

The evening meal was smaller. We had dried sausage, jerky or maybe fish. Sometimes we had Salzgurken (salted cucumbers) and almost always Butterbrot (butter bread).

The early German settlers made dried sausage using preserving techniques they brought with them from Germany. Making sausage the old-fashioned way is still a tradition in the Hill Country, although not as common as it once was.

Many sausage recipes are written in German on brittle pieces of paper and lovingly passed down through the generations. Sausage-making day in the fall is a family gathering and a celebration, with lots of laughter, beer and Gemütlichkeit.

There are fundamental steps in the art of sausage making, although the techniques and the ingredients vary from one family to another.

Henry Borchers's Sausage Recipe

20 pounds meat, ⅔ deer meat and ⅓ pork
¾ cup salt
½ cup coarse ground black pepper
2 tablespoons saltpeter
Garlic and red pepper, to taste (optional)
Casings (beef or pork intestines)

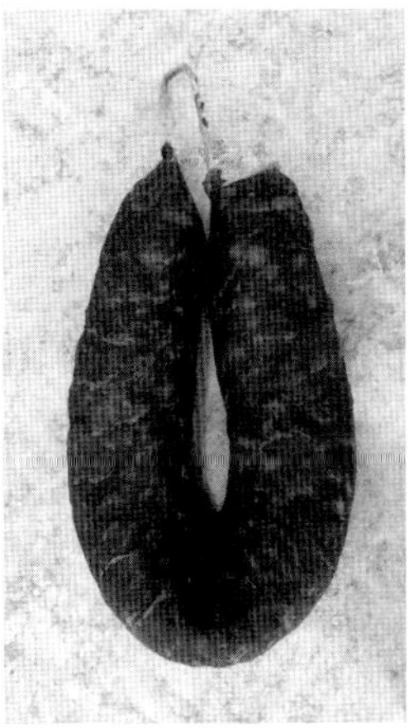

A ring of dry deer sausage. *Austin Klaerner.*

The pork is necessary because deer meat is lean and tough. By itself, deer meat is rather bland. Adding ground fatty pork makes the sausage juicy and adds to the flavor.

First debone and cube the deer meat and pork. Mix the cubed meat together in a large pan or tub. Then add the seasoning. (Some sausage makers add garlic and red pepper to taste.) Mix the meat and the seasoning thoroughly using your hands, and grind it through a course plate. Mix thoroughly again and grind again with a finer plate.

The meat is now mixed, ground, seasoned and ready for stuffing.

Cut the casings into strips about 15 inches long, and soak them in warm salt water. Tie one end of the casing with a string and slide the other end over the stuffing nozzle. Feed the meat into the casing, letting the casing slide through your hand as it fills with sausage. Pack the casing tight enough that no air gets inside but not so tight that the casing breaks. When the casing is full, tie off the other end with the string to make a ring.

After the casings are stuffed and tied, hang the rings in the smokehouse. Smoke the sausage about four hours, using oak wood for flavor. The sausage absorbs the flavor of the smoke. Let the sausage rings hang in the smokehouse until reaching the desired hardness. Make sure the rings do not touch each other. Keep the area free of flies and insects. In a week or so, the sausage is ready to eat.

President Lyndon Johnson was a big fan of deer sausage. He gave rings of dry sausage to his Washington colleagues for Christmas gifts. When West German chancellor Konrad Adenauer and Admiral Chester Nimitz stayed overnight at the LBJ Ranch in 1961, Lady Bird served "a typical breakfast of eggs, deer sausage, home-cured bacon and homemade bread."

Many families made jerky at the same time they made sausage. Some people made "clothesline jerky," cut into thin strips like bacon, cured and hung to dry on a string or wire similar to a clothesline.

The Oestreich family jerky recipe called for deer meat cut into small chunks and placed in a container holding four gallons of water. The water contained about a cup of salt (enough to float an egg) and four teaspoons of pink curing salt. The recipe says to soak the meat for about four hours, drain the water and add pepper to the meat. Then string it up, smoke it and let it cure with the sausages.

Other German foods that made the most of the "waste nothing" rule included Schwartenmagen, Blutwurst, Kochkäse, Panhas and Salzfleisch.

Schwartenmagen, also called head cheese, originated in Europe, probably during the Middle Ages. It is a cold cut made with meat from the head of a calf or a pig, although variations exist throughout the world. The process takes several days. Despite the name, Schwartenmagen is not a cheese and has no dairy products. Madeleine Oestreich described the process for making it.

> *In the fall, my family would butcher a hog. At the same time, we made Blutwurst, Leberwurst and Schwartenmagen.*
>
> *We made Schwartenmagen with heart, liver and kidney meat. We even used the rind (pigskin) and ears after we boiled them and scraped them clean. We cooked the meat in an iron pot over a fire, coarsely ground it and stuffed it into the pig's stomach ["Magen" is German for stomach] after we turned the stomach inside out and made sure it was clean. We tied one opening of the stomach with a string, stuffed the ground scraps inside, tied the other opening and cooked the whole thing again in the pot.*
>
> *Then we compressed the stomach (by laying a heavy object on top) to force out the liquid. We left it overnight. After it dried, we cut it into strips. It was like a cold cut.*

Blutwurst is German blood sausage made from pork blood, fat and scraps of meat. The blood of a hog is mixed with a meat filler until it is thick enough to solidify when cooled. In Europe, the mixture often contained barley or some other grain. In Germany, Blutwurst is typically made from pork rind (skin), blood, barley and spices (similar to boudin). Most Hill Country Blutwurst is blood and meat without the grain. Madeleine Oestreich explained,

> *We collected the blood in a large container. The blood had to be constantly stirred to keep it from clotting. We mixed the blood with other pieces of meat and stuffed it in a casing to make Blutwurst.*
>
> *We cooked the Blutwurst in the same pot with the Schwartenmagen. We cooked it over a low fire. You didn't want the water to boil. When the Blutwurst floated to the top, it was done.*
>
> *Some people like Blutwurst. It's an acquired taste, I guess.*

Kochkäse (German cooked cheese) began as a way for Germans to preserve leftover dairy once it started to go bad. In the days before refrigeration, dairy had to be cooked to extend its life. Kochkäse is a semiliquid sour milk cheese that can be served on bread or eaten like a dip with crackers. It is another example of letting nothing go to waste.

Madeleine Oestreich described the process for making Kochkäse.

> *My mother poured clabbered milk in a cheesecloth sack, squeezed out the liquid and hung it on the clothesline. After it dried, we crumbled the curds in a pan, seasoned them with salt and mixed in a little baking soda so they would ferment. Then we added butter and a little milk and cooked them slowly until they were the consistency of cheese dip. You could serve Kochkäse cold or room temperature. We always ate it with Butterbrot and dried sausage. It was delicious.*

In Europe, the Germans made Panhas, or German scrapple, with coarse buckwheat. Since the early settlers in the Texas Hill Country did not have buckwheat, they used cornmeal instead. Madeleine Oestreich explained,

> *We made Panhas using water, cornmeal, garlic powder, sage, thyme, flour, salt, pepper and leftover scraps of meat. We put that all in a pan and cooked it while stirring constantly until it thickened into a mush. Then we would refrigerate it overnight. The next morning, we would slice it and fry*

> *it in a skillet, cooking it until the slices were brown on both sides. It was especially good with syrup.*
>
> *When we butchered a hog there was still some meat left on the bones. So we brined the bones in salt water for a couple of days until all the meat fell off. Then we drained the water and cooked the meat to make Salzfleisch [salt meat]. My mother served Salzfleisch with Sauerkraut.*
>
> *We made Sauerkraut by putting shredded cabbage in a five-gallon stone crock filled with salt water. My mother would put a dinner plate on top of the cabbage to weigh it down and keep it all under water. It sat there for days. When the cabbage smelled so bad nobody would come into the house, it was ready.*

Although the dish is not German in origin, quite a few German cooks in Fredericksburg made chow-chow—a vegetable relish associated with the American South. Chow-chow may have come into the country with the Cajuns of Louisiana. Another source says there could be a connection between chow-chow and the Chinese rail workers of the nineteenth century. It may have migrated to Fredericksburg with Southern Anglos in the 1850s and '60s.

"We made chow-chow from cabbage, green tomatoes, onions and carrots," Madeleine Oestreich explained. "We used whatever was left over from the garden at the end of the growing season."

Cooks diced the vegetables and cooked them in a pot with salt, sugar, vinegar and mustard. The finished product is salty, tangy and slightly sweet. It can be eaten by itself or used as a condiment. A lot of households canned chow-chow to be eaten in the winter.

Canned vegetables and dry sausage were fine for ordinary meals, but on special occasions, like small parties or Kaffee-Kraenzehen (coffee circles—Kaffee-Klatsch, as they are sometimes called), the menu kicked up a notch. Hostesses served Schmierkäse (cream cheese) with thick yellow cream, wild plum jelly, watermelon jam, homemade bread and fresh butter. For dessert, the hostess served Mandelbrot (almond bread), Pfeffernuesse (pepper nuts), Zimmetsterne (cinnamon stars), Lebkuchen (German gingerbread), Kaffeekuchen (coffee cake) and "ein Glaeschen Wein" (a glass of wine).

Weddings, birthdays and major holidays called for an all-out German feast. On those occasions, when all the hungry relatives showed up at the same time, the host family might "roast a porker," bake a turkey or sacrifice a goose. Sides included bowls of homemade noodles, Irish and sweet potatoes, rice with a topping of cinnamon and sugar and bean salad.

On special occasions in the early twentieth century, cooks made herring salad by mixing boiled smoked herring with diced beets, hard-boiled eggs, pickles, apples, Irish potatoes and vinegar, all properly seasoned.

Pickled or smoked herring had been a staple in the German diet since medieval times, as a snack or as a main course. After being cured in salt and brined in vinegar, herring could be packed in barrels and shipped long distances. The dish is often called Bismarck herring in Germany because the statesman Otto von Bismarck was so fond of it. Pickled herring, with its long shelf life, could be shipped to towns far inland, like Fredericksburg, where the Germans of one hundred years ago seemed to have a special craving for it.

Three meals a day weren't enough for those family banquets of a century ago. In the late afternoon, everyone made an extra trip to the dining room for "four o'clock coffee."

At that hour, the hostess reset the table with platters of sliced dry sausage, bread, butter, Schmierkäse (cream cheese), Kochkäse (cooked cheese), Hand Käse (ball cheese), cakes and cookies. "Four o'clock coffee" allowed friends and family members to stuff themselves one last time before the trip home. No one went away hungry.

The following dishes are some of the traditional recipes brought from Germany to the Texas Hill Country and handed down through the generations. Some of the recipes have been modified to fit more modern methods of preparation. They are from the *Fredericksburg Home Kitchen Cook Book*, 12th edition, published by the Fredericksburg Parent-Teacher Association.

Rouladen [Beef Rolls]

Cut 2 round steaks about ¼ inch thick. Then cut each steak into 3 by 5 inch slices.

Cut off the pieces close to the bone and reserve.

Spread slices on a board and pound.

Sprinkle salt and pepper on one side.

Then spread with mustard and sprinkle on bits of bacon and onion.

Roll and fasten with a toothpick or thread.

Brown roulade and small meat pieces in oil in a pressure cooker.

Remove to bowl. Drain most of fat, add 1 cup of water to loosen drippings.

Insert rack into the cooker, and replace meat.

Cover and cook at 10 lbs. pressure for 25 minutes after control starts to jiggle.
Quick cool under faucet. Remove meat, keep warm.
Remove rack. Add enough water to drippings to make 1½ to 2 cups.
Add flour/water mixture and boil until thick. Season if needed.
Pour over rouladen and serve with mashed potatoes and red cabbage.
Serves 6 to 8.

Sauerbraten [Angry Roast Beef]

Place a 3 lb. chunk of beef roast in a bowl.

Add ½ cup vinegar, ½ cup water, 1 small onion, 2 bay leaves, 3 whole cloves and 2 tsp. salt.

Cover and refrigerate at least 24 hours, turning the meat several times to marinate all sides.

Remove meat, strain and reserve liquid.

Place meat in a roasting pan and bake at 325 degrees F.

When partly done add reserve liquid and bake until done.

Use pan liquid to make gravy, adding water if necessary.

Warmer Kartoffelsalat [German Potato Salad]

Boil 7 large potatoes in jackets.

Peel and dice the potatoes when warm.

Fry ½ lb. of bacon to light brown.

Remove half of the bacon grease.

Add 1 medium diced onion to the remaining bacon grease and sauté 2 minutes.

Stir in the potatoes until all are coated.

Dissolve 1 beef bouillon cube in hot water and add 1½ tbsps. vinegar, salt and pepper.

Mix into the potatoes. Let stand in warm place for 2 hours. Stir occasionally.

May be prepared the day before and heated before serving.

Serves 6 to 8.

Wienerschnitzel [Breaded Veal Cutlet]

Cut 2 lbs. of veal round steak into 6 serving pieces ½ inch thick and tenderize.

Season with 1½ tsp. salt, ½ tsp. pepper and coat with flour.

Slightly beat 3 eggs and dip the steaks in the eggs.

Carefully coat with breadcrumbs. Let stand 10 minutes to seal coating.

Fry cutlets in shortening or oil at medium heat.

Turn cutlets several times without piercing, until brown on both sides (about 3 or 4 minutes).

Remove with tongs to absorbent paper. Serve with lemon slices.

Makes 6 servings.

Hasenpfeffer [Rabbit Stew]

Marinate 6 lbs. of rabbit meat for 24 hours in a mixture made of 1 cup red wine vinegar, 2 cups red wine, ¼ cup sugar, 2 large onions, 1 garlic clove, 2 sprigs parsley, 1 tsp. ground allspice, 1 bay leaf, 1 tbsp. salt and ½ tsp. ground black pepper.

Remove from marinade, pat dry and dredge in flour.

Brown in ¼ cup of butter.

Strain marinade, pour over rabbit and bring to a boil.

Reduce heat, cover and simmer for 1½ hours.

Thicken sauce with flour before serving.

Rotkohl [Red Cabbage]

Heat 2 tbsps. margarine in a large saucepan.

Sautee 1 medium sliced onion and 1 peeled, cored and sliced apple for 3 to 4 minutes.

Add 1 cup of water, ½ cup of red wine vinegar, ½ cup of sugar, ½ tsp. salt, ¼ tsp. pepper, 2 whole cloves and the juice of ½ lemon.

Stir and bring to a boil. Add cabbage. Cover and simmer for 45 minutes or until tender.

Serves 6.

Salzgurken [Salt Cucumbers]

Soak fresh cucumbers in salt water overnight.
Drain and wipe dry. Heat 1 gallon of water to a boil.
Fill jars with cucumbers and cover with hot liquid. Seal.

Gefüllte Nudeln [Filled Noodles]

To make the noodles:
Mix 2 eggs, 2 tbsps. water, ½ tsp. baking powder and 1 cup flour to make a stiff dough.
Roll out thin on a floured board and cut into 4x4 inch squares.
Makes 12 to 14 squares.

To make the filling:
Dice one small onion.
Sautee onion in 1 tbsp. of shortening until transparent.
Add ¾ pound of ground beef, season with salt and pepper and cook until white. Do not brown.
Drain and divide among squares.
Fold squares over and pinch edges together.
Drop into boiling sauce and cook 15 to 20 minutes uncovered.

To make the sauce:
Mix 2 cups water, 2 cups canned tomatoes, 1 tbsp. butter, ½ tsp. salt and 1 tsp. chili powder.
Bring to a boil and simmer 20 minutes before adding noodles.
Drop in noodles and add enough hot water to cover noodles.
Makes about 4 servings.

Biersuppe [Beer Soup]

Scald 2 cups of milk. Do not boil.
Mix 2 tsps. cornstarch with ½ cup of sugar and 3 egg yolks.
Blend thoroughly before stirring slowly into the milk.
In a separate pan scald two cups of beer and combine with the milk mixture.
Add 1 tbsp. sugar to 3 beaten egg whites and heap by tablespoon on top of soup.
Serves 4 to 6.

Kartoffelpuffer [Potato Pancakes]

Peel and grate 4 or 5 medium potatoes. After spooning the excess liquid from the grated potatoes, mix in 1 tbsp. minced onion, 1 egg, 2 tbsps. flour, ½ tsp. salt, ¼ tsp. hot pepper sauce (optional), 1/8 tsp. nutmeg, 3 tbsps. butter. Mix thoroughly.

Drop by scant ¼ cupful into 1 tbsp. of hot butter in a skillet over medium heat. Spread flat with a spatula. Fry until golden brown on both sides. Add more butter as needed for frying.

May be mixed in blender, starting with the egg, then diced potatoes and the rest of the ingredients.

Delicious with applesauce, peaches, other prepared fruit or syrup.

Serves 4 to 6.

The German immigrants brought to Fredericksburg a tradition of locally-sourced food, thriftiness and centuries-old preserving techniques. Those traditions formed the foundation of Hill Country German cooking for the next century.

Chapter 6

It's Risky to Criticize the Cook

He was a bold man who first ate an oyster.
—Jonathon Swift

The earliest public eateries in Fredericksburg were hotels, saloons and camp yards. The best guess is that those eateries served typical German fare, family style. Another guess is that the quality of the food varied from pretty good to barely edible. Like a lot of frontier food, it probably fought off the hunger pangs but wasn't known for flavor.

Those early dining establishments had no menus. The cook didn't take requests. The diner ate whatever came out of the kitchen (often a surprise) and didn't complain too much about it. It's risky to criticize the cook. You might need to eat there again.

The food in those early eateries was quick and easy to prepare—often dishes that could sit in a pot on the stove all day with very little attention from the cook. The concept of a real café or restaurant, an establishment solely to serve made-to-order food to the public, was still evolving in Fredericksburg. Besides, the idea of paying money for a meal outside the home took a while to catch on.

Evidence suggests that the Nimitz Hotel in Fredericksburg had a reputation as one of the better places for Essen und Trinken (eating and drinking). The kitchen at the Nimitz served a nice selection of beer, wine, white bread and fresh vegetables. Not even shortages during the Civil War could tarnish the Nimitz's reputation for setting a fine table, even though the coffee wasn't coffee at all (the Union blockade made it unavailable at any price) but a blend of parched sweet potatoes and toasted barley.

Local historian Julia Estill wrote that the Nimitz Hotel, "on lower Main Street, standing at the crossroads, [was] a most convenient place for travelers to stop for a substantial meal served in the same old dining room where Generals Lee and Longstreet, and, perhaps, Sydney Porter, refreshed themselves in days gone by."

On the other end of town, Heimann and Hotopp ran a saloon (the Crown Saloon) and a café (the Crown Café) in the two-story Doebbler Building at the 200 block of West Main (today the parking lot of the Fredericksburg Winery). A large open camp yard for travelers to park their wagons and stable their animals occupied the rest of the property, with stalls located along the side of the saloon.

In those days, teamsters and other travelers who might not have the money or the inclination to stay at one of the hotels in town camped outside in the yard, often sleeping on the ground under their wagons. For a fee, they could get feed and water for their horses or mules.

The old Doebbler Building had a second-story room where travelers could splurge and rent a cot for twenty-five cents a night. The fortunate traveler who could afford it could wet his whistle in the Crown Saloon and have a home-cooked meal in the Crown Café.

Lewis K. Smith took over the business in the early twentieth century, just as automobiles began scaring the daylights out of horses and chickens on Main Street. As late as 1919, Smith ran "an up to date café and a clean camp yard." An ad for Smith's business in the *Fredericksburg Standard* stated, "Teams get clean stalls, clean feed troughs and clean water troughs." As to the quality of people food, by necessity a secondary matter, the ad simply said, "You are getting your meals at the best eating place in town."

Over time, eateries in Fredericksburg evolved from extensions of saloons and camp yards into places that just sold food and drinks. At first, cafés served simple foods like chili, stew and chicken and dumplings—foods kept in a large pot or pan and reheated just before serving.

As the idea of cafés and restaurants caught on, the quality of the food improved, service progressed and menus expanded. Refrigeration changed the game because food could be kept safer and longer. Refrigeration also allowed cafés and restaurants to offer a greater variety of foods.

Because traditional German food was never widely popular (and much of it took a lot of time to prepare), the food offered in Fredericksburg cafés and restaurants soon shifted away from traditional German dishes toward the more popular American and Mexican cuisines. The people in Fredericksburg probably got all the German food they wanted at home. When they ate out, they wanted something else. German food never disappeared from menus entirely, but by the 1930s, only a few restaurants in town served authentic German dishes.

Not only German food but also German beer disappeared from local menus. Fredericksburg had several breweries in the late 1800s, but soon after the beginning of the twentieth century, the big beer companies in San Antonio intentionally flooded the market and put the local brewhouses out of business.

German cuisine also suffered from discrimination. During World War I and World War II, many Americans unfairly shunned things German, including food, out of a false sense of patriotism. A half century slipped away before German American culture received the respect it deserved.

As years passed, more contact with the outside world made the German culture in Fredericksburg less distinct. English slowly replaced German as the dominant language. Prohibition put saloons out of business as well as the old German beer halls where entire German families in Fredericksburg once spent Saturday and Sunday afternoons. The anti-German atmosphere in the country kept the German culture muted.

Only in the 1960s and '70s did the rest of the country put aside its anti-German feelings. In Fredericksburg, beer gardens made a comeback, and German food regained a measure of popularity. The non-German world recognized the German culture as something to be admired and celebrated.

The restaurants and drinking establishments along Fredericksburg's Main Street reflected those mood swings and cultural shifts.

KLAERNER'S CAFÉ, OPERA HOUSE AND BAR

John Klaerner ran Klaerner's Café, Opera House and Bar in the early twentieth century (where the Palace Theater Building is today). Walter C. Klaerner later owned the business. Not much is known about the food there except that it was probably short orders served to customers waiting for the show at the opera house.

SCHAEFER HOUSE CAFÉ

Heinrich "Henry" Schaefer, born in Germany in 1854, immigrated to Gillespie County, Texas, after the Civil War. He worked a farm on South Grape Creek near Stonewall.

In 1915, Henry had the artistic foresight to build the two-story red-brick Schaefer House Building at 232 East Main Street in Fredericksburg (today Vaudeville). Each floor of the building has a covered porch that looks out over the street, and there is a massive cellar below ground level.

The building formally opened on December 26, 1915, with a splashy "Grand Opening Ball" in the big room upstairs. For several years, the local Casino Club rented the ballroom for thirty-five dollars a month for its regular meetings, dinners and dances.

Not long after the formal opening of the building, a new business moved into the first floor. An ad in the January 29, 1916 edition of the *Fredericksburg Standard* announced, "A new café opened in the Schaefer Building for the dispensing of short order meals under the management of Mr. Paul Schliesing. The ladies' entrance to the café will be on the north side of the

The Schaefer House Building, 232 East Main Street. *Author's photograph.*

building and is reached through the alley adjoining Mrs. Richter's residence [the Domino Parlor]."

The article made no mention of the men's entrance, but it is presumed the gents came and went through the front door. The new business, called the Farmers Home Café, gave "special attention to family trade and dinner parties."

Business at this early Fredericksburg café exceeded expectations, and in December 1918, Henry Schaefer and his son Alfred (Fred) took it over. They renamed it the Schaefer House Café. Fred ran the business while his father tended the farm in Stonewall.

Then, in 1921, Henry and the rest of the family moved to town. They lived on the second floor of the Schaefer House Building, at the same time renting several upstairs rooms to boarders. The Schaefer House Café occupied the first floor of the building except for the west corner, which housed a barber shop.

Fred Schaefer operated the Schaefer House Café until he moved to San Antonio in 1931. For the next thirty years, he was a band and choir leader, jazz musician and restaurateur. He built Schaefer's Tavern, a popular German restaurant and drinking establishment, at 1002 North New Braunfels Avenue in San Antonio.

Meanwhile, Henry took over the Schaefer House Café when his son Fred moved to the Alamo City. In 1939, Henry opened a skating rink in the basement.

A series of owners ran the Schaefer House Café in the early 1950s, including Herbert Friesenhahn and Ransleben and Becker. In 1954, Harry and Lydia Seelig took over the business; they ran it for seventeen years until Harry's death in 1971.

Throughout its history, patrons found the Schaefer House Café a comfortable place for breakfast, lunch or dinner. An article in the *Fredericksburg Standard* (May 7, 1969) described the relaxed, easy atmosphere of the old eatery as one of "pleasant informality, with a conversation piece, an old-time bar, set against one wall."

Running a café, then as well as now, meant hard work with long hours. Operators spent most of the daylight and evening time at the café, then hurried home for a little shut-eye before opening up the next morning hours before the chickens.

Harry and Lydia Seelig served breakfast, lunch and dinner six days a week. The menu included steaks, seafood, hamburgers, sandwiches, salads, Mexican food, coffee, tea and beer. The café closed at three o'clock in the afternoon on Sundays after serving a lunch special of baked turkey and ham.

Mr. and Mrs. Franklin Loth bought the Schaefer House Café in 1971, but the business closed a few years later. By then, the tired old building needed a facelift. Bill Wareing, a Houston stockbroker, bought it in 1975 and restored it to its former grandeur.

Starting in the 1980s, the building housed the Gallery Restaurant. The grill, located on the first floor, served Continental cuisine, German dishes and Italian pasta made fresh every day. The Garden Room became a special events center that overlooked a New Orleans–style courtyard. The Blue Room on the second floor served duck, quail, veal and lamb chops.

Today, the Schaefer House Building is home to Vaudeville Boutique and Restaurant. It is one of the most elegant buildings along Fredericksburg's historic Main Street.

CITY CAFÉ

In 1916, Alfred Grobe operated a fruit stand at the corner of College Street and the Llano Road in Fredericksburg. Six years later, Grobe moved his business to a building at 106 East Main, across the street from the southeast corner of Market Square (next door to the Fredericksburg Publishing Company—where Zertz Boutique is today).

After a short time in the new location, Grobe, on a whim, set up some tables and chairs and began serving chili. (He may have been inspired by the Chili Queens of San Antonio, who sold bowls of chili for ten cents in Alamo Plaza.) Grobe called his new business a "restaurant, refreshment and fruit stand." Citizens of Fredericksburg simply called it Grobe's Chili Stand. An ad in the *Fredericksburg Standard* described the restaurant as a "sanitary short order house."

In 1923, Alfred Grobe installed electric fans in the restaurant, and he built a beer garden in the back. Advertisements in the local paper advised customers to "Bring your families and enjoy your leisure hours." The café sold fresh keg beer (near beer because of Prohibition), pies, pretzels, ice cream, cakes and all kind of short orders. The business remained open until midnight.

That same year, Grobe began advertising his business as Grobe's Café and Fruit Stand, giving the café top billing. "Don't get mad at your wife because she can't cook," the ad in the *Fredericksburg Standard* read, suggesting that the food at Grobe's was as good as a home-cooked meal and a lot less trouble.

Customer service at Grobe's Café was ahead of its time. "We will wait on your car," an ad read, "or we will serve you cold lunches and fresh keg beer from the bar."

In addition to his duties at the café, Alfred Grobe served as the local agent for the Union Bus Company. Cars—and, later, buses—left Grobe's Café four times a day for San Antonio, twice a day for Mason and once a day for San Angelo. The bus company supported the café, as passengers often arrived hungry and thirsty after a long bus ride.

Then, in November 1923, Alfred Grobe sold the café to Felix Klaerner, who had worked as Grobe's chili cook. Another investor was Major Alfred Petsch, a local attorney and state representative. After the sale, Grobe moved to San Antonio. For the next fifteen years, he owned and operated the fish market at the city market house.

The new owners of Grobe's Café in Fredericksburg announced they would operate the new business as the City Café. It would be a Fredericksburg institution for the next thirty years.

Advertised as "Fredericksburg's Best Eating House," City Café, centrally located on Main Street, was Fredericksburg's most popular eatery for years. In the 1920s, a diner could eat lunch for forty cents, dinner for fifty cents and a hamburger anytime for ten cents.

City Café also served catfish, corndogs, chili and barbecue. Locals knew they could always get a bowl of chicken and dumplings, a house specialty. City Café made and served tamales (called Nimitz Hot Tamales) as early as 1928—an indication of the popularity of Mexican food.

City Café had a Ladies Waiting Room and a Men's Wash Room. By 1930, the owners had installed ceiling fans and air-conditioning by Frigidaire. The café billed itself as "the coolest place in town."

In the beginning, City Café bought its meats and vegetables directly from local vendors (just like the farm-to-table restaurants of today), but economics soon forced the business to buy from out-of-town wholesalers. That move touched a nerve with some of the local suppliers, who remembered all too well when, a few years earlier, the big breweries in San Antonio put all the local beer makers out of business. To retaliate for the loss of revenue, some unhappy suppliers intentionally spread rumors about unsanitary conditions at City Café.

The rumors struck a chord with the public because cleanliness and food spoilage were big concerns in those days before refrigeration and regular

City Café advertisement. *Fredericksburg Standard.*

inspections by the Health Department. It is likely that some people got sick from eating in some of those early cafés.

In big cities like New York and Chicago, health inspectors began grading cafés and restaurants according to their compliance with health and safety regulations and requiring each eatery to display its report in the front window.

The owners of City Café in Fredericksburg knew that a café could only stay in business if it earned the public's trust. Owners wanted to set the record straight on the subject of cleanliness. The following letter appeared in the March 1, 1924 edition of the *Fredericksburg Standard*:

> *In attempting to give the public the best article and the best service for the price, it became necessary for us to buy everything wholesale. As a result a number of our community have been getting even by using the handy little "hammer" in attempting to ruin our reputation. We have suffered no damages. Knockers never hurt anybody but themselves. Their efforts to ruin always result in added blessings. But for those who do not know, we would say: We have established an eating place where every plate, glass, knife and every other article is thoroughly sterilized in hot water before same is used.*
>
> *The food served by us is only of the very best. Our place of business is scrupulously clean and attractive.*
>
> *We have an eating house to which any city, even three or four times as large as ours, could point with just pride.*
>
> *In conclusion, we merely want to add that your criticisms, friendly as well as unfriendly, are always welcome to our ears.*

By 1928, City Café had purchased an automatic dishwasher, an electric watercooler, an electric slicing machine, a toaster, a water softener and a Frigidaire Electric Refrigerator, allowing the café to keep a supply of clean, fresh oysters and lessening the danger of spoiled food.

In a 1931 advertisement, the City Café billed itself as "the best in the city. All machinery electrically operated. All dished sterilized. Clean and up-to-date.

"Hot tamales made in our own kitchen daily. Always fresh 'frozen' fish on hand. Fresh water catfish, 40 cents a pound, head and skin off."

On Thanksgiving, City Café sold holiday turkey dinners for sixty cents a person. "Will cost you a $1.50 in the city," the advertisement read. The café also served homemade cake and ice cream. Kallenberg's Pharmacy made the ice cream and delivered it to customers at City Café.

For part of its history, the City Café never closed. "With their all night service at their place of business," the *Fredericksburg Standard* reported, "the City Café has also installed a 'free watch' service for the sleeping public. If you have no alarm clock and want to get up any time during the night, ring the café the night before, and they will be glad to wake you up at the time you request."

Felix Klaerner sold City Café to Alex Frantzen in 1945. Frantzen remodeled and enlarged the building.

City Café closed in the 1950s. The Hill Country Community Press bought the building to house its printing equipment.

METROPOLITAN CAFÉ

In January 1920, brothers Felix and Gregor Blanchard opened the Metropolitan Café in the A.L. Patton Building at 232 West Main in Fredericksburg. Ads in the *Fredericksburg Standard* described the new eatery as "a place to eat so different. Short orders at all hours. Special dinners on Sundays and holidays. Fresh fish every Friday" in addition to "all kinds of pies, cakes and pastry."

"The most beautiful and coolest café in town" another ad proclaimed, "is now slashing the high cost of living by cutting the prices."

The Metropolitan went all out for Thanksgiving, serving a dinner that included roasted turkey, oyster dressing, cranberry sauce, Waldorf salad, au gratin potatoes, asparagus on toast, French peas, pumpkin pie, plum pudding and ice cream. In a phrase likely never heard before in Fredericksburg, the Blanchard brothers asked diners to "call ahead for reservations."

In February 1921, the Blanchard brothers announced the business would be moving to the Meurer building (the old Buckhorn Saloon building at the corner of Main and Crockett Streets), but before owners could make the move, the restaurant went bankrupt.

THE MANHATTAN CAFÉ

Like some of the earlier Fredericksburg eateries, the Manhattan Café operated in conjunction with a "cash and carry" grocery business. The exact location of the Manhattan Café is a mystery (same for its first owner), but Durst and Durst bought the business in 1921. An ad in the *Fredericksburg Standard* assured the public that the new owners ran "a first-class clean café."

Durst and Durst sold the business to the Pohler Brothers, who sold it to Frank Seiter in March 1922.

Advertised as a "Pure Food House," the Manhattan Café sold a curious assortment of ready-to-eat, early-twentieth-century junk food, including deep sea oysters, smoked bloaters (ungutted herring, salted and cured in brine—the kind immortalized by Charles Dickens), pickled herring, pickled pig's feet, pickled shrimp and just plain pickles. Jack Roeder managed the Manhattan Café until it closed sometime in the late 1920s.

TRAVELERS CAFE

The Travelers Café (sometimes spelled Travellers Café) was a well-known eating place in Fredericksburg for most of the twentieth century. Alex Mittendorf opened the café in 1924, located in the middle of the 100 block of West Main Street, next door to Klaerner's Opera House, in the heart of the business district.

In 1926, Mittendorf moved the business a few doors east to 152 East Main Street, next door to the Palace Theater. The local newspaper described the Travelers Café as "a special attraction in Fredericksburg and the Hill Country."

In the 1920s and '30s, the menu at the Travelers Café listed German, American and Mexican food, regular and short orders. Specialties included chicken dinners, boiled ham, fresh oysters and tamales "made daily in our kitchen." The café offered a daily lunch plate for forty cents, with coffee advertised as "the best in town."

A local character named Albert "Buttercup" Raute worked as a dishwasher at Travelers Café for over forty years. He lived in a room above Stehling Brothers store. One day in 1969, some friends went to check on him when he didn't show up for work. He had died in his sleep.

In 1960, Alex Mittendorf sold the Travelers Café to Victor Sultemeier. Otto Zimmermann bought the café from Victor Sultemeier in 1965. In 1968, Zimmermann sold the café to Ken and Sue Zan Braeuer.

Before buying the Travelers Café, Ken Braeuer managed the Winn's Store in Fredericksburg. He and his wife, Sue Zan, also owned the Kuntry Fried Chicken franchises in Fredericksburg and Boerne. Braeuer credited "an interest in good food and in the love for cooking that led him to the restaurant business."

The Braeuers started off with a bang. They sold four hundred turkey dinners on their first day as the new owners.

Ken and Sue Zan Braeuer served German food including Wienerschnitzel, Sauerbraten and Fleischrolladen (meat rolls)—all served with Bratkartoffeln (pan-fried potatoes)—and Rotkohl (red cabbage), homemade Brot (bread), dessert and a choice of tea, coffee, beer or champagne. The café's central location and its menu made the business, despite its name, very popular with the locals.

When the Braeuers bought the café in 1968, Fredericksburg was changing. More and more tourists passed through town. In response, the Braeuers expanded the menu to include steaks, fried chicken, grilled chicken breast, hamburgers, sandwiches, salads and other American dishes while continuing

Above: Traveler's Café, 152 East Main Street. *Gillespie County Historical Society*.

Right: Traveler's Café advertisement. *Fredericksburg Standard*.

to serve the old tried and true German food some of the locals expected. The café also offered seafood two or three times a week.

Simple furniture, school green walls and brown linoleum floors complemented the warm and informal atmosphere of the place. Originally seating about forty, over the years, the size of the dining room increased. By the 1970s, the Travelers could seat two hundred.

The Braeuers made Travelers Café famous for Wurst (sausage) with Sauerkraut, Rotkohl (red cabbage), Schweinkoteletten (pork chops), fresh baked donuts, pies, apple strudel and homemade bread. The owners bought an oven that could bake 140 loaves of bread at one time.

On the first weekend of deer season, Travelers opened at four o'clock in the morning to serve an "all you can eat" Hunters' Special Breakfast of eggs, homemade sausage, bacon, ham, grits, donuts, homemade biscuits and coffee for $1.43.

Every Sunday from eleven o'clock in the morning to two o'clock in the afternoon, Travelers Café served an "all you can eat" chicken and sausage buffet for $2.25 ($1.50 for children). The buffet came with salad and fresh garden vegetables.

In addition to dining in, patrons could order food to go. The café offered a catering service for special events.

The café had a very popular delicatessen that sold pan sausage, link sausage, dry sausage, smoked jerky, sauerkraut salad, homemade bread, pastries, Ribbon Cane Syrup and other Fredericksburg treats. Tourists could buy Texas Bluebonnet seeds, jackrabbit milk, handmade dolls, clowns and other trinkets made locally.

In 1974, the Travelers Café celebrated its fiftieth anniversary. A 1977 article in *Travel and Leisure Magazine* noted,

> *The Hill Country of Central Texas is a region set apart from the rest of the state in geography and atmosphere....For the traveler who would like to sample the atmosphere of these towns, the Hill Country is accessible on a one-day car trip from Austin or San Antonio. A very real lure of this area is the excellent cooking.*
>
> *In a long green valley of the Pedernales, not far from Johnson City, is Fredericksburg, settled by German families in 1846. The TRAVELER'S CAFÉ, at 152 East Main Street, offers Wienerschnitzel, Sauerbraten and locally made Wurst with red cabbage, sauerkraut salad, German potato salad or pan-fried potatoes. Each plate is only $2.95.*

Travelers Café was the oldest eatery in Fredericksburg when it closed in the 1970s.

TOURIST CAFÉ

Mr. and Mrs. Herman C. Hoffmann opened the Tourist Café in the 1920s. Mrs. Hoffmann ran the business. She would put coupons in the newspaper. That coupon and fifteen cents would buy a plate lunch at the Tourist Café.

In 1930, the business moved from its location at 231 East Main Street (the Kleck Building) to a new location at 151 East Main Street (across the street from the Palace Theater). The new, more central location had a horseshoe-shaped lunch counter that could seat thirty. Including tables, the new establishment had seating for fifty.

Edwin Tatsch bought the Tourist Café in October 1941. In those years, the café never closed. The menu included short orders, regular orders, hamburgers, sandwiches, chili, tamales, beer and cold drinks. Newspaper ads guaranteed "Good Wholesome Food" and "the coldest beer in town." The café sold Texas bottled beer for eighteen cents—two for a quarter.

Elmo Baethge bought the café from Edwin Tatsch in 1946. Before going into the restaurant business, Elmo worked for his father, Willie Baethge, at the general store and post office in Doss.

The Tourist Café closed in 1959. In 1960, Mr. and Mrs. Norman J. Dietel opened Das Glockenspiel Restaurant at that location.

THE MEXICAN INFLUENCE

A sizeable Mexican population lived in Fredericksburg at the beginning of the twentieth century, although the roots of that community date to a much earlier time. Outnumbered by the Germans and ignored by many historians, the Mexicans exercised considerable influence in Fredericksburg and the Hill Country.

Mexican citizens lived for the most part in two segregated areas on the edge of Fredericksburg. The Germans called those areas Mexican Town. One housing area developed where Cave Creek Road (Ranch Road 1631) crosses Baron's Creek. Another concentration of Mexican dwellings sprang up along what is today South Milam Street, south of Baron's Creek, south of an addition once called Schultzgarden.

With two vibrant societies (German and Mexican) living side by side, the two cultures naturally blended. Mrs. E.O. Meusebach, daughter of the Nimitz Hotel builder Charles Nimitz (and daughter-in-law of

Fredericksburg founder John Meusebach as well as an aunt to Admiral Chester Nimitz), recalled that in her youth, well before 1900, the orchestra playing German polkas and Strauss waltzes at the Nimitz Hotel was a Mexican family named Cruz.

Over time, the mix of Mexican and German music produced a new art form. The Germans brought the button accordion from Germany to Texas. The Mexicans borrowed that instrument and used it to create a form of music called Norteño—a unique South Texas–based music tradition that is a blend of Mexican music and German polkas, schottisches and waltzes.

The cultures of Mexico and Germany also shared food. Fredericksburg Germans ate chili and tamales prior to the twentieth century. Later, hybrid foods like stuffed jalapeños (jalapeños cut in half and stuffed with cream cheese and bacon bits) became popular in some German households. German tacos (a German sausage covered in sauerkraut and wrapped in a tortilla) are still popular at festivals.

Mexican food itself is a blend of Native American, Spanish, French and African influences. Before the arrival of the Europeans, the Mayans and the Aztecs of what is today Mexico and Central America ate beans, maize (corn), tomatoes, chocolate, avocados, chili peppers, squash, sweet potatoes and peanuts. The meat in their diets came from small wild game.

Dishes like tacos, burritos, tamales, carnitas, menudo and pozole, dishes we know as traditional Mexican food, developed when the Spanish added beef, pork, wine, garlic and onions to the Mayan and Aztec diet. In the twentieth century, a mixture of traditional Mexican food and South Texas influences produced nachos, enchiladas, fajitas and other Tex-Mex specialties.

Chili, a popular food in early Fredericksburg cafés, is a signature Tex-Mex dish. It first became popular in San Antonio after the Civil War. By the 1880s, chili queens hawked steaming bowls of chili con carne (chili with meat) for ten cents from their colorful food stands in San Antonio's Market Square and Military Plaza. Queens served San Antonio chili at the 1893 World's Fair in Chicago.

The blending of the food cultures went in both directions. In the 1890s, a German immigrant from New Braunfels named Willie Gebhardt capitalized on the growing popularity of chili. He moved to San Antonio and began selling his own brand of chili powder. Although traditional Mexican cooks despised it, Gebhardt's premixed chili powder was a hit. By the 1950s, the Gebhardt Mexican Foods Company marketed its products all over the United States and in nineteen foreign countries. The success of Gebhardt's helped popularize Mexican food.

El Gallo Mexican Restaurant, 11807 West Highway 290. Harper, Texas. *Author's photograph.*

Representatives of Gebhardt's would occasionally come to Harry Priess Grocery in Fredericksburg and demonstrate Mexican cooking. To go along with those demonstrations, the store offered special prices on cans of Gebhardt's chili and beans, spiced beans and tamales.

The Hill Country German savored Mexican food. Chili and tamales appeared on the menus of some of Fredericksburg's more popular eating establishments on Main Street in the early twentieth century.

As Mexican food became more popular, so did the restaurants that devoted themselves exclusively to it. F. Cancino (possibly Frederico or Fred Cancino) operated one of the first restaurants in Fredericksburg devoted exclusively to Mexican food. His eatery dates to at least 1935.

By the 1960s, Mexican food had gone mainstream.

The popular El Gallo Mexican Restaurant, owned by Mrs. Cipriana Arizola, opened on the corner of Main and Elk, across from the Sunday House Motel, in March 1968. The menu included enchiladas, chili, chalupas, guacamole and other Mexican dishes.

In 1969, El Gallo moved to the Security State Bank Building at 108 South Crockett Street. In 1976, the restaurant moved again, nine miles out the

Harper Highway to the Spring Creek location next to Klein's Hall, where it is still doing business today.

Julie Arizola ran a Mexican restaurant called Los Compadres on the Llano Highway in the 1980s and '90s.

BLOWING SMOKE

Barbecue (just one of its many spellings) is another food that migrated to the Hill Country from somewhere south of the border. The word "barbecue" likely came from *barbacoa*, a word with Caribbean roots that referred to not only the meat cooked over an outdoor pit but also the method used to cook it. One theory says that Mexican vaqueros brought barbacoa north to Texas, where cowboys tongue-twisted the word into "barbecue."

The word "barbecue" first appeared in print in Galveston newspapers in the 1850s. By 1890, the word had traveled on horseback to the Texas

The big three: brisket, ribs, sausage and the fixings. *Author's photograph.*

panhandle, where cowboys used it to describe a large outdoor meal featuring beef cooked on a pit at the Goodnight Ranch east of Amarillo.

Real honest-to-goodness Texas barbecue is meat (chicken, mutton, cabrito, beef or pork) cooked in some way by natural wood coals. In the Czech Belt of Central Texas, the barbecue is smoked. In the Hill Country and West Texas, the wood (mesquite or oak) is cooked down to coals in a firebox and then transferred to a pit. The meat is cooked on the pit directly over the hot coals without a flame. West Texans call it "cowboy barbecue." Anything else, as they say, is just grillin'.

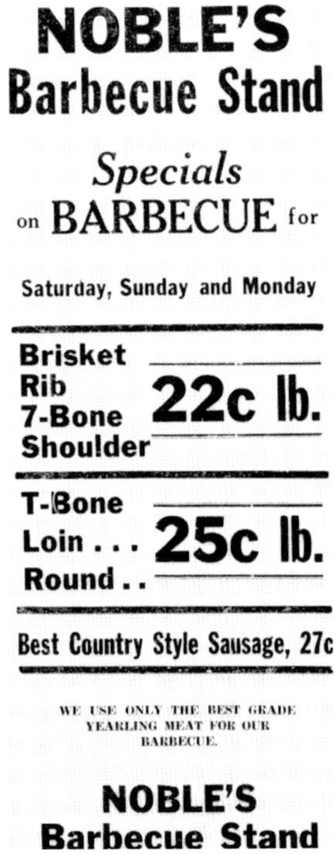

Noble's Barbecue Stand advertisement. *Fredericksburg Standard.*

No one knows who sliced the first delectable burnt end off a quivering hunk of charred brisket, but barbecue in the Texas Hill Country likely evolved just as it did in many other places across the southern United States. What seems fairly certain is that Hill Country barbecue owes its beginnings in part to a long tradition of pit-style cooking (likely with Mexican origins) and early-twentieth-century meat markets that needed a way to get rid of meat that hadn't sold by the end of the week.

Cooking meat outdoors on a pit has been going on in the Hill Country since long before anyone can remember. Ellen Maury Slayden, wife of Congressman James Luther Slayden, mentions having "barbecue" on a trip to Fredericksburg with her husband in 1907. Rainy weather in Fredericksburg forced the cancellation of a free barbecue planned for the Eisenbahnfest (the celebration of the arrival of the railroad) in November 1913.

Families in Fredericksburg had been cooking meat on a pit in the backyard, and calling it barbecue, since the 1800s. Alfred W. Noble took the next step. He built one of the first commercial barbecue stands in the Hill Country.

Born in Arkansas, Noble married Christine Hartmann of Fredericksburg in 1921. He worked for Piggly Wiggly Food Stores before opening his Fredericksburg barbecue stand in 1935.

Noble's Barbecue Stand occupied the Safe-Way Fruit Store Building at 323 East Main Street (today Auslander)—the first eatery in a long line of cafés and restaurants at that location. The business had an inside dining area, with the barbecue pit next door to the building.

Business boomed from the very beginning. Demand, especially on Sunday, exceeded supply, prompting the owner to take out an ad in the *Fredericksburg Standard* (August 8, 1935) apologizing to disappointed customers for running out of barbecue and promising to meet their demands.

"We have enlarged our barbecue pit," the ad read, "and will be able to supply barbecue to all of our customers for their Sunday meals."

The menu at Noble's Barbecue Stand listed what many people in Texas consider the "big three" in haute cuisine: barbecue, beer and ice cream. Varieties of barbecue included brisket (Noble's was one of the rare places that served that future delicacy), rib and shoulder for twenty-two cents a pound and T-bone, loin and round for twenty-five cents a pound. Country-style sausage sold for twenty-seven cents a pound and barbecue sandwiches for a nickel. Customers could eat in the dining room, or Alfred would wrap the meat in butcher paper for take-home.

Noble's Barbecue Stand opened for lunch on Saturdays, Sundays and Mondays. Many families would go to church on Sunday morning and pick up lunch to go at Noble's Barbecue Stand. Cars lined up down the block.

After Alfred Noble died in 1938, Mrs. Noble sold the business to Alfred Reeh.

BIRCK'S BAR-B-Q

"My dad learned to cook barbeque as a youngster," said Milton Birck, son of Hill Country barbecue pioneer Emil Birck. "His family made barbecue at home. I'm not sure when they started, but they'd been doing it for a long time. They burned the wood down to coals in a hole in the ground. Then they cooked the meat on wire mesh above the coals."

In Fredericksburg, early-twentieth-century meat markets picked up on the idea and began cooking their leftover meat in pits and selling it to the public as barbecue. Crenwelge's Meat Market (Mason Highway), Henke's Meat Market (Main and South Lincoln) and Fredericksburg Lockers (US Highway 87 South) all made barbecue.

"Francis Heep at Fredericksburg Locker's (today Opa's) made barbecue every Wednesday and Saturday," Milton Birck recalled. "Francis and Ben Henke made it out of the meat they couldn't sell. People stood in line to buy it."

In 1938, Emil Birck began cooking barbecue on an outdoor pit at his Conoco station at the curve on the Austin Highway in Fredericksburg. Four years later, he bought the Gulf Station at the corner of East Main and Elk Street. He continued to make barbecue at his new location.

"He had a barbecue pit under a tree next to the gas station," Milton Birck remembered. "Arthur Dietz did a lot of the cooking. There were six picnic tables next to the pit. People could eat there or take it home."

Emil Birck's pit barbecue earned a following. Business grew. People stopped at the gas station for barbecue and even bought a little gasoline.

In 1950, Emil Birck built a small enclosure with six tables, called Birck's Lunch Room, next to the gas station. He expanded in 1954 and 1956.

Then, in 1966, Emil Birck built his restaurant at 504 East Main Street in Fredericksburg. Birck's Bar-B-Q had a down-home country atmosphere. From the parking lot, the building looked like a red barn with a windmill out front. The light fixture in the entrance began as a wagon wheel.

But Birck's wasn't a joint with a few mismatched tables and rickety chairs. Once inside, customers discovered a comfortable, modern restaurant, with air-conditioning and a western atmosphere. It seated 150 in the main dining room and 125 more upstairs in the banquet hall.

Two indoor nine-by-twelve-foot stainless steel pits occupied a large space in the kitchen, with two more outdoor pits in a screened-in area attached to

Birck's Bar-B-Q, 504 East Main Street. *Bernice Burg.*

the building. Altogether, the pits could cook three thousand pounds of meat at one time.

"We served beef, chicken, sausage and ribs," Milton Birck explained. "Clinton Klaerner at Crenwelge's Meat Market made the sausage."

"We also served mutton—one of the few places that did. We bought five sheep every week from a guy in Comfort and had them butchered at Crenwelge's."

Today, brisket is the most popular cut of meat to get the barbecue treatment (the pièce de résistance of the barbecue pit), but brisket is relatively new to the menu in the Hill Country. Early barbecue in Fredericksburg could be just about any hunk of beef or pork, but not brisket.

"We put brisket in sausage," said Milton Birck. "We didn't cook brisket by itself until people from Austin and San Antonio came in and asked for it. That was in the 1970s."

"The first thing I learned is that brisket is hard to cook. I would brown it on both sides and then finish cooking it with the lean side down. At first it was hard to know when the meat was done. You just had to learn from experience."

Evidence suggests that the Jews introduced brisket to Texas. They served it on Jewish holidays, especially Passover. There was not much demand for brisket, so it became an economical option for poor Jewish families in Europe and America. The details of how this Jewish import became the Holy Grail of Texas barbeque are still to be determined.

In recent years, the popularity of barbecue has exploded. On weekends, hungry carnivores stand in line all morning for a plate of brisket at some of the trendier barbecue establishments. Food Channel superstar Aaron Franklin sold barbecue out of a truck in East Austin before smoking his way to the top of the food chain.

And barbecue is big business all over the country. Yelp lists at least forty barbecue joints—in Manhattan.

By the twenty-first century, a funny thing happened. Barbecue, once dismissed as low-class hick food, became fashionable. After decades of hiding in the shadows, this once-humble outdoor dish slipped into the house through the back door, but even then, it took a while for it to be invited into the formal dining room.

PIONEER MILLS

Millers were important people in frontier communities. Using special imported grinding wheels, millers ground wheat, rye, barley and corn to make cornmeal and flour. The Germans of Gillespie County used the cornmeal and flour to make bread, a staple in their diet.

Carl Hilmar Guenther, born in Germany on March 19, 1826, served an apprenticeship as a miller. As a young man, he left Germany for the thrill of frontier life in America, becoming one of the first millers in the Texas Hill Country.

He landed in New York in 1848, and after a short stay, he traveled to Wisconsin. Later he sailed down the Mississippi to New Orleans, then by steamship to Indianola on the Texas coast. He walked to San Antonio and then New Braunfels but decided to make his way to the new German settlement of Fredericksburg.

When Guenther came to town in 1851, the citizens of Fredericksburg rolled out the red carpet. Germans loved their bread, and now they would have a good supply of flour to make it.

Guenther bought land along the banks of Live Oak Creek, where he built an earthen dam and a millhouse. The site of Guenther's mill is just south of the Live Oak Creek bridge on Highway 16.

Guenther made the wooden gears and other working parts of the mill, but French craftsmen carved the millstones, the best money could buy, from

C.H. Guenther homestead on Live Oak Creek, Fredericksburg. *Author's photograph.*

a special kind of quartz found only in France. The millstones came to the Texas coast by ship and then to Fredericksburg by ox cart.

When running, the mill came alive with moving parts. The ponderous wheels and gears sprang to life with a surge of power that made the entire millhouse shudder.

Soon after establishing himself in business, Guenther married Henrietta Dorothea Pape from Fredericksburg.

Guenther's business thrived for the first few years, but in 1859, a drought hit the Hill Country. The Pedernales puddled up, and Live Oak Creek went bone-dry. With no water to turn the wheel, Guenther's mill stood still as a tombstone.

The drought convinced Guenther he had to find a more reliable power source. So he sold his place in Gillespie County and bought property in San Antonio a mile south of the Alamo. He built a mill powered by the San Antonio River and one of the first houses in what is now the King William District.

Guenther's company struggled at times until the railroad came to town and solved the grain supply problem. And with the coming of the railroad, markets extended far beyond the range of ox carts and horse-drawn wagons. By 1885, sales exceeded Guenther's wildest dreams.

In 1898, the business incorporated under the name C.H. Guenther and Son Inc., using the trade name Pioneer Flour Mills.

Time has washed away every trace of Guenther's mill on Live Oak Creek, but Pioneer Mills is still doing business in San Antonio. Its sales territory covers twenty-two states in the South and Southwest. Many of its products, including Pioneer All Purpose Flour, are on the shelf at HEB grocery stores.

C.H. Guenther's company is one of the oldest continuously owned family milling businesses in the country. Corporate offices are at 2201 Broadway in San Antonio. Dozens of Guenther's descendants are shareholders in the company.

RISING TO THE OCCASION

The Germans brought a love of fresh bread with them from Germany to the Texas Hill Country. Housewives baked bread at home until a string of bakeries in Fredericksburg began making loaves of fresh bread for families, stores and restaurants.

Bread-making takes a lot of time. Because the shelf life of bread is short, housewives of the early twentieth century typically made bread several times a week.

Lillian Hahn, age ninety-five, still makes bread at her home in Fredericksburg but now uses a bread machine. ("I can't knead it anymore," she says.) She shared with me her Oma Wilke's recipe for making bread.

> *My Oma Wilke (Emma Borchers Wilke) would dissolve 2 packages of dry yeast in a quart of warm water. Then she mixed in 5 tablespoons of sugar, 2 tablespoons of salt and 8 tablespoons of melted shortening. Next she added 3 or 4 cups of flour. As she mixed, she added flour as needed (up to 11 cups). She kept mixing and adding flour until the dough was just the right consistency. It had to be smooth and elastic but firm and not sticky to the touch.*
>
> *She covered the dough and let it rise until it doubled in size. She punched it down and let it rise again. She punched it down again, kneaded it (usually 8 to 10 minutes) and cut it into 3 equal parts. She put those 3 parts in 3 greased bread pans and let the dough rise again. Then she baked the 3 loaves for an hour.*
>
> *My mother made bread the same way. It was hard work, and it took most of a day.*

Considering the time involved in making bread, it is easy to understand why a housewife would choose to save herself hours of work by purchasing a loaf of fresh bread at the bakery for ten cents.

In 1891, Franz Moritz and his wife, Katherine (Stein), opened a bakery in Fredericksburg. They had recently moved into town from their farm on Palo Alto Creek. Franz had previously worked in a bakery in Galveston. He ran the bakery in Fredericksburg until about 1913.

Beginning in 1916, M. Tichmann operated a bakery in the Louis Priess Building at 141 East Main Street. Tichmann made bread, cakes and pies "of the finest quality." Fruitcake for Thanksgiving became a specialty.

Tichmann originally called his bakery Fredericksburg Bakery (he may have bought an already established business by that name), but he changed the name to Tichmann Bakery. The business took orders over the phone and delivered anywhere in town.

A notice in the *Fredericksburg Standard* (May 5, 1917) announced, "On account of the high price of flour and other materials, we will have to charge 10c for a loaf of bread, beginning Tuesday, May 8th, but we will make the loaves bigger. Tichmann Bakery."

George Stucke bought Tichmann Bakery in 1917. Stucke came from San Antonio, where he had operated a bakery on Commerce Street for ten years. Some sources say Stucke purchased the Louis Priess building in 1923.

Except for a brief period, Stucke ran the Fredericksburg Bakery until his death in 1948. Three years before he died, he finally joined the twentieth century, giving up his wood-fired oven for gas.

Werner Schult from Harper opened a bakery in Fredericksburg on June 21, 1924, in the Wahrmund Building (sometimes called the Clark Building) at 312 East Main Street (today Der Lindenbaum).

Schult sold the business to Ed Stark in 1927. Stark called it the Blue Bonnet Bakery. He opened a second bakery up the street, next door to the Palace Theater.

In 1928, H.N. Kissel bought Blue Bonnet Bakery and changed the name to City Bakery. Werner Schult took the business back in 1929. Schult then sold the bakery to William Moellendorf later that year. Moellendorf had bakery experience in Gonzales, Luling and San Antonio.

Schwiening's Bakery opened in the spring of 1930. The newspaper described the location of the bakery as being "the second door next to the Post Office."

In 1932, three bakeries on Fredericksburg's Main Street cranked out bread within a few blocks of one another: Schweining's, Moellendorf's and Stucke's. A customer could buy a loaf of bread for a nickel.

In 1939, William Moellendorf sold his bakery to his brother-in-law Theo Dietz. Theo, born in Gillespie County in 1880, was an experienced baker, having operated bakeries in Kerrville and Kingsville. The Dietz family ran the legendary bakery for the next seventy years.

In 1965, Dietz Bakery, now owned by Theo's son Edgar, moved up the street to 214 East Main Street. When Edgar retired, his son Don ran the bakery.

Dietz Bakery made white bread, French loaf, rye, whole wheat, pumpernickel and a local favorite known as pull-apart. Dietz made pull-apart by baking two loaves of white bread together, then pulling them apart, leaving a crusty "heel" at one end of each loaf. Customers lined up down the block to get it, hoping the bakery didn't run out before they got to the counter.

The white bread had a chewy golden crust with a soft inside. The pumpernickel, made from coarsely ground rye berries, was dark and hearty. There are quite a few locals still around who remember walking home cradling Dietz bread—the loaf wrapped in white paper, still warm from the oven.

Many people, myself included, remember the aroma of Dietz Bakery more than anything else. The morning air was almost edible. It lured

Dietz Bakery Building, 214 East Main Street. *Author's photograph.*

customers to Dietz's door, drawn by an irresistible force. Those same people remember a sign behind the counter, put up by the ladies who worked there, that read, "I only work here because I'm too old for a paper route, too young for Social Security and too tired for an affair."

The actor Jack Webb once stopped into Dietz Bakery. Arkansas governor Winthrop Rockefeller had Dietz bread flown to the governor's mansion in Little Rock.

Dietz closed in 2010. I can still hear the weeping.

In the 1950s, Bruce and Dorothy Scully opened Fredericksburg Bakery in the old Louis Priess Building next door to Dooley's. The bakery made pastries and homemade bread. Some of the recipes went all the way back to George Stucke in the early twentieth century.

Once lured through the front door, a hungry customer couldn't resist a delicious Guglehupf, Stollen (coffee cake), long john (lemon-filled donut) or Dutch apple pie.

Mike and Patsy Penick bought the bakery in the 1980s. The business closed in 2014.

BLUE BONNET CAFÉ

In 1930, E.F. Heeson and Louis Wehmeyer welcomed the first customer to the Blue Bonnet Café in the Kleck Building, 231 East Main Street, in the building formerly occupied by the Travelers Café. Mr. Heeson managed the business. His motto was "a clean kitchen." Prior to opening the Blue Bonnet, Mr. Heeson worked at the Wolf's Inn Café in San Antonio—a well-known chicken dinner restaurant near the corner of Wurzbach and Fredericksburg Road. The Blue Bonnet Café in Fredericksburg had a short history and soon closed.

BRIGHT STAR CAFÉ

Edwin Petmecky opened the Bright Star Café in the Maier Building (corner of Main and Adams) in 1935. The café offered short-order lunches "prepared in the most modern and sanitary manner."

The early menu listed sandwiches for ten cents, two hamburgers for fifteen cents, a small bowl of chili for ten cents, a large bowl of chili for fifteen cents, a cold Dutch lunch (an individual serving of sliced cold meats and cheeses) for twenty-five cents, a schooner of Sabinas Beer (brewed in San Antonio) for five cents and a twelve-ounce bottle of Sabinas for ten cents. The list of drinks also included local and imported wines.

After several changes in ownership and management, the business closed in the 1940s.

OAK GROVE HUT

In 1937, William Hoffmann and Edgar Mosel launched the Oak Grove Hut on the San Antonio Highway (US Highway 87 South), next door to the Oak Grove Service Station. The eatery sold barbecue, hamburgers, sandwiches, cold beer and other refreshments. Customers could eat indoors or outside on picnic tables under the shade trees.

Oak Grove Hut didn't need to advertise in the newspaper. The sweet-smelling smoke from the barbecue pit drifting all over town was the best advertisement money could buy.

Every Sunday, customers lined up after church to buy barbecued beef, mutton, chicken and sausage—for dine-in or take home. The Oak Grove Hut also did custom barbecuing.

The business closed in 1976. A part of the Opa's Sausage plant now occupies the site.

DOWNTOWN CAFÉ

Alfred Reeh opened the Downtown Café on May 13, 1939. Formerly Noble's Barbecue Stand, the business sold barbecue beef and sausage by the pound, barbecue sandwiches, side orders, chili, beer and ice cream. The opening day special included a barbecue sandwich and a beer for ten cents. For most of its history, the Downtown Café stayed open twenty-four hours a day. It closed in 1946.

WHITE HOUSE CAFÉ

In 1946, Mr. and Mrs. Lawrence Meurer opened the White House Café (formerly Downtown Café) at 323 East Main Street in Fredericksburg (where Auslander's is today). Before opening a café, Lawrence Meurer worked in the wholesale restaurant supply business in San Antonio.

When the Meurers bought the business, they completely remodeled the interior of the building. At the same time, they upgraded the kitchen with new butane-powered kitchen equipment.

The White House Café specialized in fried chicken, homemade sausages, T-bone steaks and hot lunches. The bar sold beer and wine.

On December 22, 1951, Mr. and Mrs. Meurer sold the White House Café to Cecilia Hannemann. Hannie's Cafe sold lunches and short orders, but it closed after a short run.

SUNNYSIDE HUT

At first glance, the year 1933 may not seem like an ideal time to start a business. The Great Depression had just hit the Texas Hill Country like a

Joe Louis right hand. Both Fredericksburg banks defaulted in 1932. The unemployment rate rose to levels never experienced before. The economy was a mess. No one had money.

But Walter and Mary Hollmig believed in the future, so they opened a restaurant in the middle of the worst financial crisis in history. To survive, they learned to be thrifty and creative in attracting customers.

Mary Hollmig named the business Sunnyside Hut. The name expressed her optimism and cheery disposition.

The original Sunnyside Hut, a small wooden building where Broadway Bank stands today, had no indoor dining. Customers walked up or drove up and ordered through the window. Then, in 1941, the Hollmigs added on to the building, providing space for a small indoor dining area, restrooms and cold storage. Sometime in the evolutionary process, Walter and Mary hired carhops for the convenience of the drive-up customers.

By 1945, the dining area had a few tables, a Wurlitzer jukebox and a Skee-Ball game. Adults played dominoes in the back of the building. The position of the domino table took advantage of occasional blasts of artic air from the walk-in cooler.

Sunnyside Hut, 204 West Main Street. *Gillespie County Historical Society.*

Sunnyside Hut menu. *Gillespie County Historical Society.*

But drive-up customers provided most of the business. Cars would pull up in front of the building in the shade of a large canvas awning. Carhops would take orders and deliver the food to the driver in his car.

Sunnyside Hut served what has become standard fast food fare, including burgers, fries, hot dogs, sandwiches, enchiladas, fountain drinks and ice cream. Walter Hollmig created the ice cream in a room in the back of the building next door that today houses the Nevins Law Firm.

In addition to standard fast food fare, the kitchen turned out a mean T-Bone steak, and the bar served ice cold beer on tap or in the bottle.

Sunnyside Hut jumped ahead of the curve in other ways. Customers could phone in their orders and have their food delivered to their homes or businesses free of charge.

Until it closed in 1961, Sunnyside Hut was an important hub of community life in Fredericksburg. Teenagers gathered there after home football games, dances or the movies. Walter and Mary Hollmig welcomed teens, despite that annoying adolescent fad of stealing salt and pepper shakers. Parents took younger children there to celebrate special events and as a bribe for good behavior. If children showed good manners at church or at Oma's house, parents took them to Sunnyside Hut for ice cream.

Sunnyside Hut was a cool oasis on a hot Texas day at a time when air-conditioning was just catching on. "The Frosty Root Beer at Sunny Side was sugar sweet and ice cold," a former Fredericksburg teenager told me, "and the beer was the coldest in town."

SUNNYSIDE TAVERN

Walter and Mary Hollmig built the Sunnyside Tavern in 1937. Customers could find "Fredericksburg's newest and most modern dining and dancing establishment" on Highway 87 South (the new San Antonio Highway), just outside the city limits. The Hollmigs opened with a free dance featuring Bob Schmerbeck and his orchestra.

The dining room, soda fountain and restrooms occupied the front of the building. Tables and chairs in back could seat one hundred people around a forty-by-thirty-four-foot polished Maplewood dance floor. Some weekends, the music was live. Other weekends, the patrons danced to the "toe-tickling tunes of the foremost orchestras reproduced on phonograph records."

Sunnyside Tavern, now the VFW Post 7105, 710 South Washington Street. *Author's photograph.*

Mary Hollmig assured the public that the Sunnyside Tavern would be "a modern place of clean entertainment." She and Walter enforced strict discipline at all times.

Sunnyside Tavern sold hot dogs, hamburgers, steaks, sandwiches, fried chicken, beer, soft drinks and ice cream. Patrons could eat outside in the breeze under the big awning ("as cool as a river bank") or inside in air-conditioned comfort.

The Veterans of Foreign Wars (VFW) bought Sunnyside Tavern in 1968. The building is now home to VFW Post 7105.

La Mesa Café

Customers could find the La Mesa Café inside the old Ostrow Hotel that once stood at 239 West Main Street (the parking lot of the Fredericksburg Winery). The entrance and dining room had a Spanish motif, and neon lighting added a modern decorative touch. The business opened in 1945.

In the beginning, the business operated cafeteria style (offering select dishes from an open counter). Customers had a choice of two meats, potatoes, gravy, two vegetables, desert and drink for fifty-five cents.

Then Werner Burrer and August Ahrens bought the business on April 1, 1946. Burrer, a recently discharged serviceman, managed the café. He served in the U.S. Army for forty-three months— forty-one months overseas in the Pacific Theater as a mess sergeant. Before the war, he worked as a cook at City Café. He later operated the Schmokhaus Bar-b-que Stand.

The new menu at La Mesa Café included chili, tamales, enchiladas, T-bone steaks, hamburgers, sandwiches, donuts, homemade pies and cold bottled beer. Customers with a taste for German food considered the Wienerschnitzel and Sauerkraut "Das Beste."

Later, Sam and Mary Ann Klaerner ran Mary Ann's Coffee Shop there prior to opening Klaerner's Café on Highway 87 South.

Security Café

Security Café opened next door to the Security State Bank in the remodeled Plaza Hotel building (205 West Main Street) on January 28, 1941.

Fredericksburg's newest eatery was air-conditioned and offered "home cooked meals and fine steaks." Mrs. Martha Heimann was the proprietress. House specialties were chicken dinners and chicken and dumplings.

The owner decorated the interior of the café in blue with a blue tile lunch counter and matching table covers. Seating capacity was fifty-four.

Later, Sam and Mary Ann Klaerner ran the Security Café prior to opening Mary Ann's Coffee Shop. The Security Café closed in the 1960s.

THE OAKS CHICKEN SHACK

In 1945 Otto Seipp raised the curtain at the Oaks Chicken Shack, located half a mile off Main Street on the Harper Highway. The Chicken Shack served fried chicken, steaks, sandwiches, beer and soft drinks. Seipp served barbecued chicken on Friday and Saturday evenings. The Oaks Chicken Shack closed in the 1950s.

SOUTH HEIGHTS HUT

Mr. and Mrs. Harry Schlueter threw open the doors at South Heights Hut on September 20, 1947. Located on the Austin Highway just beyond the South Heights Bridge, the new drive-in served sandwiches, hamburgers, seafood and short orders, both at tables inside and outside at the curb.

South Heights Huts offered a complete line of soft and fountain drinks, beer and ice cream. In addition to the food and fountain service, the drive-in had a jukebox and a dance floor.

Mr. and Mrs. Billy Jenschke bought the business in the 1960s. In the '70s, South Heights Hut evolved into a drive-in grocery. In December 1974, Lanell Schlueter opened a hair salon at that location.

THE SHANTY

Mr. and Mrs. Herman Petermann opened the Shanty on Highway 87 South (the San Antonio Highway) in February 1948. The Shanty was a drive-in with curb service, and there was an indoor dining room. The kitchen served barbecued beef, pork and sausage. The menu also included burgers, chicken in a basket, enchiladas, chili, tamales and beer (two beers for a quarter). The business closed in 1951.

BETTY'S RESTAURANT

In the 1950s, Kurt and Betty Burmester opened Betty's Restaurant at 323 East Main Street (across from the Nimitz Hotel, where Auslander is today). At the time, cafés and restaurants along Fredericksburg's Main Street served mostly American and Mexican dishes, but Betty's Restaurant broke new ground. The twenty-four-hour restaurant specialized in authentic German food in a Bavarian atmosphere.

The Burmesters came to Fredericksburg from Germany, so they knew a thing or two about German food.

The menu included Wienerschnitzel, Bratwurst, Rollfleisch, Sauerbraten, hot potato salad, Sauerkraut, fresh black and white breads, cold soup and a dish called Königsberger Klogs (possibly similar to Königberger Klopse—a

Auslander Restaurant and Biergarten, 323 East Main Street. *Author's photograph.*

Left: Betty's Restaurant menu cover, 1968. *Jimmy Reichenau.*

Below: Betty's Restaurant menu, 1968. *Jimmy Reichenau.*

German Foods

BRATWURST PLATE, Sausage Plate with Sauerkraut, Potato Salad or German Fries 1.75
ROLLFLEICH, Stuff Beef Roll From U. S. Choice Round Steak, Served with Red Cabbage and German Fries 2.95
SAUERBRATEN, Roast Beef (Sour) with a Special Gravy, Served with Red Cabbage, Cooked Prunes and German Fries 2.00
KOENIGBERGER KLOPS, German Meat Ball, Served with Red Cabbage and German Fries 2.25
POTATO PANCAKES, Served with a Salad and Applesauce 1.50

German Famous Schnitzel

All Our Schnitzel Are Cut From Selected Veal Tenderloin

WIENER SCHNITZEL, Special Veal Cutlet Breaded with a Special Batter, Served with Red Cabbage and German Fries 2.25
WIENER SCHNITZEL A LA HOLSTEIN, Special Veal Cutlet Breaded with a Special Batter, Served with Fried Egg and Topped with Anchovies, Served with Red Cabbage and German Fries 2.50
RAHM SCHNITZEL, Special Veal Cutlet Breaded with a Light Cream and Served with Red Cabbage and German Fries 2.50
KASE SCHNITZEL, Betty's Own Way For a Delightful Cheese Schnitzel For Cheese Lovers, Served with Red Cabbage and German Fries 2.50

Steaks

T-BONE, Juicy, Tender and Delicious 2.95 - 3.75
CLUB, It's Large, Tender and Delicious 2.95
TOP STRIP SIRLOIN, Choice Beef and Bursting with Succulent Flavor 2.95

All Steaks Above Served with Salad and French Fries

Seafoods

FILLET OF FISH 1.50
SEAFOOD PLATE, Two Shrimp, Two Oysters and Cod Fillet 1.95
DEEP FRIED JUMBO SHRIMP 1.95
FRIED OYSTERS 1.95

Served with Salad and French Fries

Fried Chicken

TENDER FRIED CHICKEN Served with A Salad and French Fries
Four Pieces 1.50
Three Pieces 1.35
Four Pieces All White 1.75
Three Pieces All White 1.55
Four Pieces All Dark 1.75
Three Pieces All Dark 1.55

WE SERVE REAL HOMEMADE BREAD AND PIES FROM BETTY'S OVENS

STEW, Homemade .80 - .95

Appetizers

HOMEMADE BEEF SOUP .50 - .65
CANNED SOUPS: Chicken Noodle or Tomato .50

Crisp Salads

LETTUCE & TOMATO .60
TOMATO .60
COMBINATION SALAD with Lettuce, Tomato, Celery, Ham and Cheese 1.00

Side Orders

All Fresh Homemade

FRENCH FRIES .35
GERMAN FRIES .45
SHREDDED HASH BROWNS .50
GERMAN POTATO SALAD .50
SAUERKRAUT or RED CABBAGE .45

Desserts

HOMEMADE PIES: Apple, Cherry, Chocolate, Blueberry, Lemon and Coconut Pies .30
ICE CREAM, Two Dips .15

From The Grill

GRILLED BONELESS HAM 1.80
PORK CHOPS with Applesauce 1.75
HAMBURGER STEAK with Onions 1.65
BREADED VEAL CUTLET, Deep Fried 1.50
CHICKEN FRIED STEAK, Deep Fried 1.50

Served with a Salad and French Fries

Sandwiches

HOT ROAST BEEF SANDWICH with Salad and French Fries 1.75

COMBINATION .80
FRIED HAM .65
CHEESE .50
GRILLED CHEESE .50
ROAST BEEF .90
HAMBURGER .45
CHEESEBURGER .60

GERMAN SAUSAGE SANDWICH 1.15

Beverages

COFFEE .15
SANKA .15
ICED TEA .15
HOT TEA .15
SOFT DRINKS Served with Ice .15
MILK, 8 oz. Glass .15
12 oz. Glass .25
MILK CHOCOLATE, 8 oz. Glass .20
12 oz. Glass .30
HOT CHOCOLATE .20
CHILLED JUICES: Orange, Grapefruit or Tomato .25

Breakfast

We Serve Grade AA Extra Large Eggs

ONE EGG with Toast .50
with Ham, Bacon or Sausage .90
TWO EGGS with Toast .80
with Ham, Bacon or Sausage 1.10
HOT CAKES (2) .50
with Ham, Bacon or Sausage .90
THREE HOT CAKES .75
with Ham, Bacon or Sausage 1.10
COFFEE with a Warm Up with Any of the Above Orders .15

ORDER HAM, SAUSAGE, or BACON .50
GERMAN SAUSAGE .50
OMELETTES, Plain 1.00
OMELETTE with Cheese, Ham, or Bacon 1.40
SHREDDED HASH BROWN .30
BREAKFAST STEAK .80

CEREALS
with Milk .35
with Cream, Half and Half .50
OATMEAL with Milk .50
with Light Cream .65

ORDER OF TOAST, Three Slices .20
HOMEMADE BREAD, Two Slices .20

BETTY'S RESTAURANT
FREDERICKSBURG, TEXAS

Prussian specialty of piquant meatballs in a white wine sauce with capers.) The bar offered a wide selection of German beers.

In addition to German food, Betty's Restaurant served fried chicken steak, fried catfish, ice cream and all kinds of desserts.

Mr. and Mrs. Elgin Usener bought the restaurant in 1969. The Useners added more floor space and the now iconic German-style turret to the front of the building.

Betty's closed later in the '70s, and in its place, Mike and Sally Clark opened the Auslander Restaurant, featuring a covered beer garden. Auslander, under new ownership, is still in business today, serving German and American food.

THE TOWER RESTAURANT

The Tower Restaurant, at 526 West Main Street, shared a low-slung, flat-roofed building with Jim's Ice House at the corner of Bowie and Main (where Bigs Convenience Store is today). The business took its name from the big water tower just up the street.

The busy kitchen cranked out hamburgers, chicken, fried shrimp and the Tower's famous fried finger steaks, while the soda fountain served malts, milkshakes, banana splits and soft serve ice cream.

The Tower offered inside dining, curbside service or food to go. Carhops took orders and carried food to curbside customers on metal trays that hung on the car door, just like in the movies. The Tower offered good food at reasonable prices. Hungry teenagers on a budget could buy a hamburger, fries and a drink for forty-nine cents. Even the Golden Arches couldn't match that.

There, in the Tower parking lot, teens hung out with friends (adults called it "loitering"), listened to music and did what fun-loving teenagers do best: strut, swagger and show off.

Squealing tires, booming radios and loud exhaust pipes added to the charm of the Tower. On a typical Saturday night, the parking lot saw more action than a three-ring circus. Sparks flew as sweethearts got together and sweethearts broke up—sometimes on the same night. As a side show, there was plenty of laughter, theatrics, trash talk and an occasional fistfight. Every Friday and Saturday night, the curtain went up on a new production—sometimes a comedy, sometimes a drama and sometimes a musical.

THE TOWER
AND
JIM'S ICE HOUSE

One-stop service for your convenience

Ernst Hoffman
WY 7-5350

James Turrentine
WY 7-2656

997-5608 **THE TOWER** 997-9790

Prices subject to change
SCHOOL LUNCH SPECIALS---ORDER BY NUMBER
No.1 Hamburger with French Fries & 10¢ drink --- .53
No.2 Grill Cheese with French Fries & 10¢ drink --- .53
No.3 Hot Dog with French Fries & 10¢ drink--- .53
Hamburger or Chiliburger --- .30 with French Fries--- .50
Jumbo Hamburger --- .45 with French Fries --- .65
Cheeseburger --- .40 with French Fries --- .60
Jumbo Cheeseburger --- .55 with French Fries --- .75
Charcoal Burger with chips --- .45 Jumbo Charburger/chips--- .65
Hot Dog --- .25 Corn Dog --- .25
Chili Dog or Cheese Dog --- .35
Coney Island --- .45
Bar-B-Q on Bun --- .50
Bar-B-Q Sandwich --- .60
Cheese Sandwich --- .35 Grill Cheese Sandwich --- .30
Bacon and Tomato Sandwich --- .45
Ham Sandwich --- .50
Ham and Cheese Sandwich --- .60
Veal Steak Sandwich --- .65
Chicken on Bun --- .50
Fishwich --- .45 with French Fries --- .65
Egg Sandwich --- .35
Ham and Egg Sandwich --- .60
Bacon and Egg Sandwich --- .60
Order French Fries --- .30 Short --- .25
Order Potato Gems --- .35 Short --- .30
French Fried Onion Rings --- .35
Hamburger Steak --- 1.30
Chicken Fried Steak --- 1.30
Breaded Veal Cutlet --- 1.30
T-Bone Steak --- 2.00
Club Steak --- 1.90
TOWER SPECIAL ---Finger Steak Basket --- 1.00
Order Fried Chicken --- 1.25
Short Order Fried Chicken --- 1.10
Order Fried Shrimp --- 1.25
Short Order Fried Shrimp --- 1.00
Order Poppin' Shrimp --- .98
Order Enchiladas --- 1.10
Short Order Enchiladas --- .85
Small Frito Pie --- .40 Large Frito Pie --- .65
Burrito --- .25 with Chili & Cheese --- .55
Pizza Pie --- 1.10

FOUNTAIN DRINKS

Coke, Dr. Pepper, Root Beer, Sprite, 7-Up ---.10,.15 & 20¢
Coffee --- .10 Tea --- .10 Milk --- .15
Sodas --- .25 Malts & Shakes --- .30 Sundaes .30
Banana Splits --- .45

KEEP IN YOUR PHONE BOOK COVER

Left: The Tower Restaurant, 526 West Main Street. *Gillespie County Historical Society*.

Right: The Tower Restaurant menu. *Polly Zenner*.

Car radios, eight-track tape players and the Tower's exterior speakers playing rock and roll from the Wurlitzer jukebox in the dining room provided the soundtrack, except for certain Saturdays in the fall when most everyone tuned in to hear the Texas Longhorns and local legend Happy Feller play football. Even Aggies cheered when Happy booted one through the uprights.

But the Tower was much more than a restaurant. It was a part of the American drive-in culture created by teenagers looking for something to do on Saturday night.

Teenagers want to be independent, and for a teen in the 1950s, '60s and '70s, independence meant getting behind the wheel. A car meant freedom. A driver's license marked the transition to adulthood.

By the 1950s, most families had cars—often more than one. Gasoline sold for twenty cents a gallon. Young people couldn't resist the call of the open road.

In towns all over America, cruising became a weekend ritual (adults called it "driving around aimlessly.") In Fredericksburg, a teen driver could easily put fifty miles on the family Chevy in one night, just cruising (some called it "dragging") Main Street, back and forth, between the Y and the Nimitz Hotel, all on a dollar's worth of gas. A part of the routine included a stop at the Tower to see if anything interesting was going on—as if anyone had to ask.

Few patrons, even the hard-core regulars, knew what it took to run a place like the Tower. The hours were long and grueling—eight o'clock in the morning to midnight, Monday through Thursday, with special late hours on Friday and Saturday.

Tommy and Polly Zenner ran the Tower from 1967 to 1974. "On Saturday nights when Pat's Hall was open, we didn't close until 2:00 a.m.," Polly told me. "After cleanup, we took the employees home. Sometimes we didn't get home until 4:00."

As the setting sun cast long shadows on Sunday evening, the Tower parking lot stood mostly empty and strangely silent, as if resting up for the next curtain call when the chaos, the comedy and the drama started all over again.

PIONEER VILLAGE RESTAURANT

In 1949, Mr. and Mrs. C.R. Conley of Houston launched the Pioneer Village Restaurant on West Main Street, at the junction of the Mason and Junction Highways, next door to the Pioneer Village Service Station. The lunchroom had a counter and eight tables. The dining area seated thirty.

The restaurant never closed. It served steaks, chicken, seafood and barbecue. The cook prepared a plate lunch each day at noon and special Sunday dinners. The restaurant offered curbside service every evening after five o'clock.

Otto and Gene Zimmermann (then operators of Sunnyside Tavern) bought the restaurant in 1951. The doors opened from five o'clock in the morning to twelve noon, except during hunting season, when the restaurant opened at four o'clock. The menu included salads, seafood, Mexican food, barbecue, hamburgers, steaks and fried chicken. The Zimmermanns also catered private parties.

Mr. and Mrs. John W. Carson Jr. bought the business in 1970. The café closed a few years later.

COUNTRY DINER

In June 1953, Bob Moritz opened the Country Diner, located a mile west of the city limits on the Mason Highway. The first floor of the building housed the restaurant. The Moritz family lived on the second floor. The Country Diner served American food. Chicken fried steak was a specialty. The business closed in the 1970s.

DELUXE CAFE

The Deluxe Café, at 905 East Main Street, across from Millers Court in Fredericksburg, served steaks, seafood, fried chicken, salads, Mexican food, hamburgers, sandwiches and homemade pies. Andrew Miller built the café in 1960 to serve locals, tourists and guests at his motel.

The café closed in the 1980s.

KLAERNER'S CAFÉ

Sam and Mary Ann Klaerner opened Klaerner's Café on Highway 87 South in 1966, but they were not newcomers to the restaurant business. Before opening Klaerner's Café, Sam and Mary Ann operated the La Mesa Café on the corner of Main and Crockett Streets and Klaerner's Café and Hotel at 239 West Main Street (southeast corner of Main and Orange Streets) in Fredericksburg.

Klaerner's Café served Mary Ann's famous chicken and dumplings, the specialty of the house, every Wednesday. The Friday special was turkey and dressing. The menu also included Mexican food, steaks, fried chicken, seafood, salads, hamburgers and homemade soups.

Mary Ann made dinner rolls, donuts and pies fresh every morning. A lot of locals made Klaerner's Café a midmorning stop for coffee and donuts.

ANDY'S DINER

Andy's Diner occupied a redwood and pink brick building at 413 South Washington Street, four blocks south of Main Street. Andy Knopp, James Knopp and Werner Knopp built the diner in 1959. Andy Knopp managed the diner. He had several years' restaurant experience at a location on the Mason Highway.

The restaurant, known for its home cooking and casual atmosphere, served steaks, salads, chicken, burgers, donuts, homemade pies, Mexican food, rolls and corn sticks. The menu even listed a few German dishes, including an Opa's Sausage plate, Wienerschnitzel and Jägerschnitzel. Cooks made all entrées, sauces, salads and desserts on-site and from scratch.

Locals gathered at Andy's for breakfast and coffee in the mornings. Wedding parties rented the private room for rehearsal dinners.

For years, the Fredericksburg Lions Club met in the back room at Andy's. In the 1970s, the Lions held their Wild Game Dinner there.

Andy's closed in 2020. Today, the building houses Campo Azul Mexican Restaurant.

Andy's Diner, 413 South Washington Street. *Gillespie County Historical Society.*

DAS GLOCKENSPIEL RESTAURANT

On April 23, 1960, Mr. and Mrs. Norman J. Dietel opened Das Glockenspiel Restaurant at 151 East Main Street (site of the old Tourist Café). Mr. and Mrs. Alfred Hoffman managed the business. The owners and managers did their best to "preserve the old world tradition of the German pioneers who settled in the area in the 1840s."

The dining room decor struck a balance between Germany and the Texas Hill Country. Eight ticking cuckoo clocks and pictures of old Heidelberg hung next to images of white-tailed deer and wild turkey by local artist Charles Beckendorf. A German flag hung on the wall next to a mounted collection of barbed wire. The face of German chancellor Konrad Adenauer hung above the doorway next to a framed letter from President Lyndon Johnson to the owner's son thanking the son for helping out on the LBJ Ranch.

Das Glockenspiel served authentic German food, "Everything from Schnitzel to Sauerbraten." While a player piano filled the room with German polkas and waltzes, waitresses in dirndl dresses served Rotkohl (red cabbage), Sauerkraut, Spaetzle (tiny dumplings), homemade Brot (bread)

Das Glockenspiel Restaurant advertisement, 151 East Main Street. *Fredericksburg Standard.*

and Feuersenf (hot mustard). Beverages included bier (keep the stein for $3.50), Sodawasser (soft drinks), Kaffee and Milch (milk).

Other items on the menu included sandwiches, hamburgers, chili, tamales, enchiladas, seafood, cold keg beer, bottled beer, canned beer, wine, champagne and root beer. An extensive German import gift shop occupied the space next to the cash register.

Das Glockenspiel, with its straightforward German food and decor, was a sign of things to come. After fifty years, German pride was back.

Das Glockenspiel closed in the mid-1960s. In 1965, Bob France operated a restaurant there called Das Gasthaus. Victor Sultemeier took over the business in 1966.

In 1970, Norman Dietel sold the building to Richard J. Potter of Dallas. Mr. Potter had recently purchased the Schreiner Mansion in Kerrville. He reopened the restaurant as the Glockenspiel. Ken Knopp managed the business. The owner had plans to use the Glockenspiel as a model for a string of German restaurants under the name Little German Inn, but the plans fell through.

SUNDAY HOUSE RESTAURANT

The Sunday House Restaurant, at 151 East Main Street in Fredericksburg, opened for business on June 23, 1967. The complex included the restaurant, a wine cellar, a coffee shop, a convention center, a banquet hall, a private club and a swimming pool.

Like Betty's Restaurant and Das Glockenspiel before it, the Sunday House Restaurant celebrated its German roots in its architecture as well as its food. The focal point of the building was an old pioneer home, built in the 1860s, incorporated into the front part of the complex.

The new restaurant's name, Sunday House, comes from those tiny homes, called Sunday Houses, that Fredericksburg is so famous for.

Dick and Ruth Molter managed the Sunday House Restaurant. They came to Fredericksburg with years of experience managing restaurants in California. Joe Pollard, the chef, had seventeen years' experience as chef at the Fort Sam Houston Officer's club and at the St. Anthony Hotel on Travis Street in San Antonio.

Diners could eat in the coffee shop, the main dining room, the small mezzanine or in the family room. Dark stained wood and white plaster

Sunday House Restaurant, 515 East Main Street. *Gillespie County Historical Society.*

adorned the walls in the dining room. The complex included a banquet hall and a private club located at the rear of the building called the Baron's Cub with its own cocktail lounge and dining room.

The Sunday House Restaurant menu listed American fare (hamburgers, sandwiches and salads), German food and a number of exotic dishes, including frog legs and Hungarian goulash. German chocolate cake topped the dessert menu. The cellar held a large selection of wines.

GAY 1890s SUPPER CLUB

On March 6, 1970, Kenneth and Sue Zan Braeuer, owners of the Travelers Café on Main Street, kicked off the Gay 1890s Supper Club and Cocktail Lounge, a members only club located at 102 North Llano Street just around the corner from the Travelers Café. The two businesses shared a kitchen.

The Gay 1890s Supper Club began with twenty-five members. That number grew to fifty by the time the business opened. By June 1972 the club had 500 members. Mr. and Mrs. Caspar Real, local ranchers with a spread between Fredericksburg and Comfort, joined as numbers 499 and 500.

The interior of the club was vintage '70s, featuring dark cedar paneling with exposed cedar beams. Red shag carpet covered the floors, except for a small tile dancefloor in front of a low carpeted bandstand. Matching red drapes framed the windows. Light fixtures were antique brass chandeliers (reproductions of old gaslights) from Kendall-Hodges in Fredericksburg. Furnishings included square tables for four with captain's chairs upholstered in black vinyl.

The main room could seat eighty-six, with a private dining room that could seat an additional thirty-five. The club served menu items from the adjoining Traveler's Café. Diners could also fire up an on-site grill for cooking steaks. Members brought their own steaks, with the Supper Club supplying the sides.

Most Friday and Saturday evenings the club served an all you can eat seafood buffet for $4.75. During high school football season, the buffet line opened before and after home games. Just for fun, the club hosted special events such as Family Burger Night, Limbo Party Night and Hot Pants Night. (Hot Pants Night lasted until styles changed—about a month.)

The bar opened from five o'clock in the afternoon to midnight (one o'clock in the morning on Saturdays), with a happy hour from five to seven o'clock every evening, offering drinks at reduced prices. Art (Shadow) Koch tended bar. Darlene Payne waited tables.

The club kept the beer in an eighteen-cubic-foot cooler behind the bar but piped it to the spigot through a fake beer keg, giving the visual effect of the beer coming from a real keg.

Live entertainment featured comedy, music and dancing every weekend. Ceasar Masse, "the Prince of the Punchline," sometimes did two floor shows a night. Then Vernon Schwartz played the organ, and Gail Seagroves played the piano. Small combos like the Latin IV (formerly the Momentos) or Tom Rhodes and His Imperials played on Saturday nights. There was no shortage of polyester.

The Gay 1890s Supper Club was a nod to a special time in the history of Fredericksburg. In the real 1890s, the Casino Club sponsored concerts, dances, plays and dinners at the Nimitz Hotel. At those events, Fredericksburg's citizens could dress in their Sunday clothes and enjoy a special evening of music, food and entertainment.

The Chase Bank Building at the corner of Main and Llano stands today at the site of the Gay 1890s Supper Club.

DOMINO PARLOR

The Domino Parlor occupied the building just east of what used to be Dietz Bakery on Main Street. The building is about 160 years old, although its earliest history is a little uncertain. It would stand for about a century before it became a restaurant.

The German Emigration Company originally assigned the town lot at what is now 222 East Main Street to Adolph Schildknecht but deeded it to Schildknecht's assignee John Schmidtzinsky in 1849. A fire destroyed the original deed in 1850.

Schmidtzinsky sold the property to J.A. Alberthal in 1858. The building we now know as the Domino Parlor probably existed then, because the purchase price of $500 seems to indicate a building stood on the property. Elise Kowert wrote in the *Fredericksburg Standard*, "In all probability John Schmidtzinsky built the front part of the house."

A little-known but fascinating feature of the building is a large cellar with a domed rock ceiling. The builder filled the cellar with a dome of sand to hold the ceiling in place until the mortar dried.

The Hermit, Peter Berg, probably built the cellar. He built one at the Keidel House just down the street. Because the cellars at the Keidel House and the old Domino Parlor are so similar, many people believe Berg built them both.

The Domino Parlor Building, 222 East Main Street. *Author's photograph.*

In 1860, J.A. Alberthal sold the building to Ottocar Mueller and Christian Frantzen for $1,100. Mueller and Frantzen operated a drugstore there. When Frantzen died, Mueller became the sole owner.

Ottocar Mueller sold the property to Adolph Dreiss in 1873. Max von Reinbach lived there for a time and operated a drugstore in the front room.

Henry Richter, born in Baltimore, raised in Virginia, bought the building in 1901. He lived in the back of the building with his wife and children and sold jewelry and musical instruments out of the front room. The bay window was Richter's show window. Richter and friends performed concerts in the front room where the music spilled out onto Main Street.

Richter played the violin, the classical guitar and several other instruments. He also composed music. He knew and corresponded with Antonin Dvorak, one of the first Czech composers to achieve worldwide recognition.

The building stayed in the Richter family until Walter Knoche bought it from the Richter heirs in 1945. For a time, it housed a Mexican restaurant. Henry Ransleben ran a domino parlor and pool hall there.

By 1970, the century-old structure needed a facelift. When Bill and Nancy Wareing bought the place in 1973, they removed the old plaster, re-pointed the rock and restored the building to its former glory.

The Domino Parlor, more beautiful than ever, reopened in 1975 as a restaurant and Biergarten. The kitchen served sandwiches, hamburgers, light lunches, salad plates, chili, homemade stew and Baskin Robbins ice cream. The bar served keg beer, bottled beer and soft drinks.

The most popular feature of the Domino Parlor was the Biergarten. Red cedar latticework formed a partial cover over the paved area. A rock ledge enclosed a native rock fountain, pool and small garden.

The Biergarten was a great place to bring the family or gather with friends after work. It breathed new life into an old Fredericksburg tradition.

OMA KOOCK'S

In 1975, Guich Koock bought the old dilapidated Krauskopf Bros. building at 312 West Main Street in Fredericksburg (today Hondos on Main) and turned it into Oma Koock's Restaurant. The importance of Oma Koock's was not just in the food it served but also in the publicity it generated and the attention it focused on Fredericksburg and good old German cooking.

Oma Koock's Restaurant, 312 West Main Street. *Gillespie County Historical Society.*

Oma Koock's made headlines around the country long before the restaurant deep-fried a schnitzel or pried the top off a longneck. The buzz surrounding the restaurant and its owner signaled an exciting new phase in the life in Fredericksburg. This small Hill Country community had been discovered. Fredericksburg was about to enter a period of growth and prosperity most small towns only dream of.

William Faulk "Guich" Koock was already a celebrity when he opened Oma Koock's in 1975. He rose to fame as one of the pranksters who bought Luckenbach back in 1970 and turned that tiny ghost town in the middle of nowhere into a country music fantasy land for the Woodstock generation and a major tourist attraction.

When asked about his unique name, Guich always said, "Daddy raised dogs, and he gave all the good names to the dogs."

In 1974, Guich's outrageous personality caught the eye of Hollywood casting director Shari Rhodes. She cast Guich as a Louisiana highway patrolman in *The Sugarland Express*, Steven Spielberg's first film.

After that, Guich went to Hollywood, where he made a career playing likeable rednecks and good ole boys. He played the trainer in *North Dallas*

Forty with Nick Nolte and Mac Davis and the TV pitchman in *Piranha*. He played Sheriff Conley in the movie *Macintosh and T.J.*, starring Roy Rogers and Joan Hackett. From 1977 to 1979, he played Harley Puckett, the goofball deputy sheriff in the sitcom *Carter Country*.

Guich's mother was Mary Faulk Koock, an Austin socialite and restaurateur and the sister of actor and storyteller John Henry Faulk. Mary agreed to help Guich with the menu at his new restaurant in Fredericksburg.

Just like Guich himself, the old limestone building he bought on Fredericksburg's Main Street was something of a celebrity. The area where the building sat had been a wagon yard in the 1870s next door to Engelbert Krauskopf's gun cap factory. Oscar Krauskopf, Engelbert's son, built the cut limestone building in 1900. Oscar sold buggies, carriages, wagon parts and farm implements.

But the magnificent old building with the large double doors and interesting cast-iron cornice needed some work before it was ready to meet the public. First, workers shored up the walls. Then Guich had Clayton Knopp build a fireplace of native limestone and soapstone. The restaurant had an antique bar, a small stage hidden by a vaudeville curtain, an outside patio and a rustic beer garden tastefully decorated with rocks, trees, brush and prickly pear.

Guich filled the shelves inside the restaurant with his eclectic collection of stuff, including an eagle wing fan, a stuffed hawk, at least a dozen animal heads, a buffalo skull, a set of deer horns he received from author J. Frank Dobie (he once worked as Dobie's driver) and an enormous unfinished oil painting.

Oma Koock's specialized in German food, just like Oma used to make. The kitchen cranked out Salzfleisch, Sauerkraut, Apfelstrudel, German potato pancakes, hot vinegary potato salad, Schnitzel and German meatloaf.

More than any business on Main Street, Oma Koock's put Fredericksburg on the map. The restaurant and its entertaining owner generated tons of publicity and became something of a tourist attraction in their own right.

At first, the restaurant opened two days a week, Friday and Saturday, but as Guich said, "Business was so good we had to close down and regroup." When running on all cylinders, Oma Koock's opened for lunch every day except Thursday.

Guich sold Oma Koock's in the 1980s. In the '90s, Andy and Genie Smith operated an eatery there called the Plateau Café.

IMMIGRANTS LANDING

In 1975, Joe and Yvonne (Von) Bolin opened Immigrants Landing at 604 West Main Street, next door to their antique shop. Joe had restaurant experience as a manager at Luby's.

A charming old building, furnished in part with Joe and Von's antiques, housed the restaurant. Diners entered through an old set of double doors. The fireplace in the dining room added to the cozy atmosphere. The kitchen served steaks, seafood and broiled chicken with wine sauce.

The Bolins had roots in Johnson City. They knew Lady Bird Johnson. Lady Bird would occasionally take her family, Secret Service agents in tow, to Immigrants Landing after church.

This new restaurant provided still more evidence that a big change was coming for Fredericksburg. Art Kowert, editor of the *Fredericksburg Standard*, could feel a new energy along Fredericksburg's tired old Main Street. He wrote,

> *Fredericksburg, long known for its many attributes that bring tourists here, has still another attraction that some may fail to realize—restaurants and eating places that serve fine foods.*
>
> *The traditional and long-established cafes all serve outstanding meals and now in recent years several new places, all with a distinctive atmosphere of their own, and fine foods to go with it, are making their mark in the community.*
>
> *The latest of these, and the one with most unusual name, is The Immigrants Landing, located on West Main Street, in the shadow of the city's water tower. It will open October 8.*
>
> *Like Oma Koock's and The Domino Parlor, this new dining place has grown out of what was once an old building that has been converted into one of the most delightful and tastefully decorated "in the decor of old Fredericksburg" structures in the city.*

ENCHANTED INN

Once upon a time, the Enchanted Inn was a cozy restaurant located near Bear Mountain, three miles north of Fredericksburg on FM 965 (the road to Enchanted Rock). Marlin Samford operated it in the 1970s and early '80s.

The kitchen served Mexican food, barbecue and the best chips and salsa around. The green sauce was especially memorable.

The restaurant closed because the owner was unable to raise the money to upgrade the sewer system. The Enchanted Inn is now a food trailer.

KEN HALL AND CO. TEXAS BARBEQUE

Barbecue made Ken Hall famous, but football had already made him a legend. In the early 1950s, he was the "Sugar Land Express," the most prolific high school running back in the history of Texas. Some of his records still stand.

Paul "Bear" Bryant recruited Hall to play football at Texas A&M. Hall then played five seasons of professional football in the National Football League, the American Football League and the Canadian Football League.

After football, Ken worked twenty-eight years in the sugar business, mostly in Southern California. Then, in 1986, Ken and his wife, Gloria, moved to Fredericksburg and opened Ken Hall and Co. Texas Barbeque on Highway 87 South.

Pitmaster Noah Hostetler used only aged mesquite wood to cook brisket, chicken, pork, ribs and sausage. Brisket was the big seller. It's the backbone of Texas barbeque. "If you can't do brisket in Texas," Ken Hall told *Texas Monthly Magazine*, "you should close the door." Available sides included beans, potato salad, coleslaw and Ken Hall's famous Barbeque Sauce—marketed in sixteen states. Gloria Hall made cakes for dessert, and Inge Hostetler made homemade pies.

In 2002, Ken and Gloria sold the business to Dan and Kala Martin. The Martins continued to make good barbeque there but under the name Cranky Frank's. The name came from the Martins' son Frank, who could be quite cranky when he was a toddler. *Texas Monthly* named Cranky Frank's one of the fifty best barbeque joints in the world. The business closed several years ago.

PLATEAU CAFÉ

Andy and Genie Smith came to Fredericksburg from San Antonio. Andy worked as a stockbroker, but he had deep roots in the Hill Country. His great-great-grandmother, Mason County legend Anna Martin, was an Old West storeowner, rancher and one of the first female bank presidents in the United States. She is a member of the National Cowgirl Hall of Fame and Museum in Fort Worth.

Andy and Genie's eatery, the Plateau Café (formerly Oma Koock's), served butterfly shrimp, grilled chicken salad, New York strip, charbroiled rainbow trout with fresh dill sauce, chicken parmesan, border bean burgers, vegetable plate, salads, Texas fried catfish and Mexican food. The dessert menu included bread pudding, chocolate cake and berry cobbler.

The Plateau closed in 2004.

Today, the restaurant is a monument to Guich Koock's partner-in-crime, Hondo Crouch, onetime co-owner of Luckenbach. Hondo's On Main serves burgers, beer, sandwiches, salads and Mexican food in a casual atmosphere. The Biergarten, with a stage for live music, is one of the most popular spots in town.

The beer garden at Hondo's, 312 West Main Street. *Author's photograph.*

JESSICA'S RESTAURANT

The menu at Jessica's Restaurant, at 102 East Ufer (corner of Ufer and South Adams), included steaks and seafood grilled over hickory, wine, beer and champagne. The patio overlooking Baron's Creek was one of the more scenic dinner locations in town.

James Lawrence later opened Baron's Bach Inn at that location.

ENGEL'S DELI

Larry and Barbara Brown opened Engel's Deli at 320 East Main Street in Fredericksburg, just west of the Nimitz Hotel. Engel's served charcoal-broiled hamburgers and thirteen different kinds of sandwiches. The deli also made a delicious fruited chicken salad, avocado stuffed with chicken salad and a fresh spinach salad. The menu included a choice of four sausage plates served with bread and your choice of potato salad, sauerkraut or red cabbage. Hungry people traveled miles to gorge on Engel's decadent homemade desserts, including apple strudel, Kahlúa cheesecake with a chocolate mocha sauce, carrot cake, chocolate pie, walnut pie, seasonal fruit pies, pecan cream cheese pie, creamy lime pie, Mississippi pecan pie, coconut cream pie and lemon meringue pie.

When Fredericksburg got too crowded, Larry and Barbara Brown moved west and opened the Square Plate in Mason.

SPANISH CELLAR RESTAURANT

Louis and Kay Sanchez-Navarro moved to Fredericksburg from Corpus Christi in 1970. The next year, they opened the Spanish Cellar Restaurant at 201 North Llano Street (the corner of Llano and Austin Streets).

The Spanish Cellar featured Spanish cuisine, which was both exciting and a little risky for a small Texas town in 1971. One of the signature items on the menu was a Spanish dish called paella, a name most Fredericksburg Germans had never seen and couldn't come close to pronouncing. Paella is a fluffy rice dish made with chicken, shrimp, sausage, peppers and other spices. The menu also included huevos rancheros (delicately poached eggs smothered in a hot pepper sauce and served on white flour tortillas) alongside a tender beef chop.

The bar at Spanish Cellar Restaurant served beer and a broad selection of wines, including Spanish wines. The stairs led to the Galerias La Giralda gift shop on the second floor.

Barbara Monkhouse took over the restaurant in 1977—a time when cowboy chic was in vogue, Texas pride was at its peak and Luckenbach attracted more visitors than the San Antonio Riverwalk. She changed the menu to focus on tried-and-true Texas dishes, including chili, enchiladas, tacos, tamales, nachos, steak, seafood and Lone Star Beer—the national beer of Texas.

Chapter 7

Beer and Wine Are Gifts from God

God has a brown voice, as soft and full as beer.
—Anne Sexton

Not to overstate this, but most Germans love beer. "There are but two things," a reporter once wrote, "interference with which will call the German-American to arms—his political equality and his beer."

While people around the world associate Germans with beer, the drink had been around thousands of years before the Germans discovered it. Beer may be the oldest drink there is—next to water. The formula for making beer is possibly the oldest recipe known to mankind.

Indications are that the Sumerians (in modern-day Iran) discovered the fermentation process, probably by happy accident. The Babylonians and Egyptians perfected the art of brewing and passed it on to the Romans. The Romans introduced beer to the Germans.

German monks have been brewing beer since AD 1,000. In fact, between the ninth and thirteenth centuries, monks were the primary producers of beer across what is now Germany.

While Germans did not invent beer, they took to it from the beginning. Today, the love of beer in Germany is stronger than ever. There are 1,300 breweries in Germany (a country about the size of California). Almost 80 percent of adults in Germany drink beer regularly. The average German consumes over 100 liters of beer every year. Only the Czechs and the Austrians drink more beer than the Germans.

To Germans, beer is much more than a thirst-quencher or a stimulant. There is a strong cultural bond between Germans and their beer. An April 1883 article in *Lippincott's Magazine* explained that "beer and wine the German looks on as gifts of God, to be enjoyed in moderation for lightening the cares of life and adding to its pleasures."

The strong attachment between Germans and beer is reflected in language. When a storm is coming or a conflict is developing, the common saying in Germany is "something is brewing." When all hope for a solution is gone, they say "hops and malt are lost," meaning the situation is hopeless.

Even beer containers are expressions of German culture. Steins are decorated in nostalgic Germanic or Bavarian themes. One theory says that beer drinkers added pewter lids during the Black Plague to prevent diseased flies from getting into the beer.

Compared to many Americans, Germans have a relaxed attitude toward beer and wine. In Germany, a young person can legally drink beer at age sixteen—before he or she can drive or vote (the age for hard liquor is eighteen). And drinking beer casually, in public, is common in Germany, particularly after work.

That said, Germans tend to be responsible drinkers. They drink in moderation. It is rare to see a German who has had too much to drink, even during Oktoberfest.

Beer had a profound effect on society, both in Germany and in the United States. The *Cincinnati Inquirer* concluded that the consumption of German beer helped civilize America.

> *Formerly Americans drank scarcely anything else than whiskey, usually very bad whiskey, and the consequence was quarreling, strife and fights. Now Americans drink almost as much beer as the Germans do, and whereas Americans used to pour everything down their throats standing, they now sit good naturedly and chat over a good glass of beer without flying into one another's hair.*

The early settlers in Fredericksburg, being German, loved beer, both for its taste and as a social lubricant. They brought the art of brewing to the Texas Hill Country.

Quite a few Hill Country Germans brewed beer at home, but in time, commercial breweries produced most of the local beer. In 1860, Texas had eleven brewhouses. By 1870, the number had grown to twenty-seven—all located in the German-populated areas. Several small breweries in

Fredericksburg supplied the needs of local beer drinkers until the big operators in San Antonio declared "Beer Wars" and put the local guys out of business.

Before a unified rail system and refrigeration, towns needed local breweries. Beer didn't travel well. It went flat in a hurry, so it needed to be brewed close to the people who drank it.

Beginning in the 1850s, Captain Charles Nimitz brewed beer in the cellar under his saloon at the Nimitz Hotel in Fredericksburg. The Civil War and the Union naval blockade dried up the supply of hops and other ingredients, so Captain Nimitz stopped brewing beer soon after the war started.

In 1857, Adolph Assig from Germany borrowed $850 from Frank van der Stucken and started a wheat beer brewery on the north bank of Town Creek in Fredericksburg.

Singing groups (Sängerbunde) who gathered periodically in Fredericksburg for singing contests (Sängerfests) especially liked Assig's brew. The singers claimed Assig's beer lubricated their voices. They drank the stuff as fast as the bartender could tap it.

Friedrich Probst came to Fredericksburg from Germany in 1857 to work as a barrel maker for Adolph Assig. When Assig moved to Blanco County in 1861, Probst took over the Fredericksburg business. Probst moved the brewery to a building in the 300 block of West Austin Street next door to his house.

Probst called his brew Probst's Special Beer. He sold a lot of beer locally, but he hauled his barrels of foamy delight as far west as San Angelo.

The Mauer brothers, Henry and John, operated a brewery in Marlin, Texas, before opening their brewhouse on Creek Street (near the Kuenemann House) in Fredericksburg in 1875. A couple of years later, Henry left for Seattle, leaving John to run the company.

In the 1890s, a group of local businessmen operated a brewery called the City Brewery, possibly out of Probst's or Mauer's abandoned brewhouse. Everyone called it City Beer.

Meanwhile, big things were happening in the brewery business in San Antonio. In 1884, the St. Louis beer giant Anheuser-Busch built the Lone Star Brewing Company on Jones Avenue. A couple of years later, a group of San Antonio investors built the San Antonio Brewing Company between Avenue A and the river a few miles north of downtown.

The Lone Star Brewing Company would soon begin brewing a popular beer called Santone. The San Antonio Brewing Company made Pearl Beer, "the beverage of the masses."

It wasn't long before the big guys in San Antonio made the decision to expand into the lucrative Gillespie County beer market. To get their foot in the door, the big guys hired teamsters to haul wagonloads of San Antonio suds to Fredericksburg, where their representatives sold it cheap to saloons along Fredericksburg's Main Street.

The San Antonio beer invasion caused a problem for the local guys. City Beer, made in Fredericksburg, sold for ten cents a glass at local saloons. Pearl sold for a nickel.

The beer wars came to a head in December 1898. That month, the *Gillespie County News* printed a letter from a group of hopping mad saloonkeepers, determined to win the beer war even if it meant losing money in the short go.

> *From this time, all the saloons which sell City Beer (brewed in Fredericksburg) will give you a big "Schooner" for five cts. We have to do this to keep up with the procession and to hold our own with those who began the battle and want to crowd us out of our trade.*
>
> *It is a battle between local capital and the capital of a northern millionaire. Will you support him or us? Support home industry and, as before, drink only what is well known to be the Best Beer in Texas—the City Beer. If you do so, you help to keep the money at home, as all the stock in the City Brewery, and all local saloons is held by local capitalists and the profits they receive are not sent north and thereby lost to the south, but are used to employ home labor and in home industries. "Live and let live" will always be our motto.*

But in the long haul, local breweries couldn't sustain the losses and couldn't compete with large corporations who sold their beer for a nickel a glass. By the early twentieth century, all the local breweries had closed up shop.

Breweries made beer, but saloons constituted the middlemen who sold it to the public. In fact, a saloon, more often than not, was the first mark of civilization on the advancing Texas frontier. It was, after all, a cheap and easy startup. A potential saloonkeeper needed only a tent, a barrel of whiskey, a keg of beer, some fairly clean cups, a couple of sawhorses, two planks for a bar and a thirsty customer with money in his pocket in order to launch his drinking establishment.

Saloons were among the first permanent buildings in new Texas towns. Frontiersmen built structures of lesser importance, like houses, churches, stores and schools, as they got around to it.

Beer and wine may have been heavenly gifts from God, but most frontier Texas whiskey came from another direction. No standards existed for making whiskey. Some of it was poison—if taken internally. When drinking shots of that early hooch, a wise old boozer often said, "One is a revelation, two is pure heaven, three is a big mistake."

Saloons not only furnished men with places to drink, fight and play poker, but they also performed an important social function as community gathering places. Drinking, after all, is best done in the company of others. It's more fun that way.

From 1850 to 1920, saloons dominated social life in small towns and big cities all over America. They were boisterous men's clubs where mostly working-class, mostly White menfolk with callused elbows and strong opinions could debate politics and argue the important issues of the day.

Saloons and politics went together like beer and bratwurst. Before some Texas counties had courthouses or city halls, men conducted city and county business in saloons.

Saloons were democratic for their day. Every White man was equal in a saloon. A thirsty patron checked his social status at the door before he bellied up to the rail to have a glass or a shot. A saloon was a beer drinker's republic where men could passionately debate the issues on a more or less equal basis.

In 1897, saloons in America numbered around 250,000. In today's terms, that's 20 saloons for every Starbucks.

In Fredericksburg, it seemed as if a saloon occupied every corner along Main Street, with several more in between. Some saloons stayed in business for years. Others stayed open for only a short time. After a brief mention in the newspaper, they closed for good.

In 1900, a lineup of Fredericksburg saloons scattered along Main Street included the Buckhorn Saloon (Hermann Ochs, owner), the Capital Saloon (owned by the Schmidt Brothers), the Bank Saloon, the Crystal Saloon, the Bismarck Saloon, Ma's Saloon (Max Wahrmann, owner), White Elephant Saloon (E.L. Kusenberger, owner), William Jordan's Central Park Saloon, Herman Lehne's Saloon and Stoffer's Saloon—a "Gentleman's Popular Resort."

A 1916 shortlist of Main Street saloons included the Buckhorn Saloon (owner: Otto Meurer), the Bismark Saloon (owner: Louis Gerhard), Capital Saloon (Schmidt Brothers, owners), the Crystal Saloon, the Farmers Home Saloon (owner: Herbert Kott), Peters Saloon and Opera House (Ed Peter: owner), Klaerner's Opera House and Bar (owned by Walter Klaerner), the

Louis Hotel and Beer Saloon (Louis Klaerner, owner) and Rudolph's Saloon (owner: Hilmar Weber).

By the early twentieth century, most saloons in Fredericksburg were selling "cold" beer for ten cents a glass, along with wine, liquor and cigars. Most saloons also served food to any customer who purchased a drink, although the quality often ranged from "not very good" to "terrible."

Most saloons in Fredericksburg had pool tables and some form of gambling. In the early twentieth century, some saloons offered games of chance called marble machines or marble boards. The White Elephant Saloon had a separate room out back where certain men played high-stakes poker.

Quite a few horse races began with a liquored-up cowboy talking trash in a saloon. In Fredericksburg, the unpaved expanse of San Saba Street (now Main Street) doubled as the racetrack.

"Many the quarter-horse I rode up and down the Main Street in Fredericksburg on Sundays," recalled Hall of Fame trainer Max Hirsch. "We raced from the Vereins Kirche to the Buckhorn Saloon."

When Texas Blue Laws ordered drinking establishments to close at midnight and on Sundays, saloons complied—sort of. The White Elephant Saloon in Fredericksburg always locked the front door at the appointed time, but the back door sometimes stayed open all night and all weekend, especially if patrons were particularly numerous and thirsty or a hot poker game was in progress.

NIMITZ HOTEL AND BAR

Making and selling beer was good business on the Texas frontier. Just before the Civil War, Captain Charles Nimitz, owner of the Nimitz Hotel on the corner of Main and Washington Streets in Fredericksburg, added a beer cellar beneath the dining room floor.

The Nimitz beer cellar turned out a respectable product. Locals as well as soldiers from Fort Martin Scott enjoyed Captain Nimitz's brew. Nimitz shipped his beer to Fort Concho, Fort McKavett and Fort Mason until difficulties obtaining grains and hops during the Civil War forced the brewery to close.

Sixty years later, during Prohibition, a reporter for the *Fredericksburg Standard*, standing in the old Nimitz beer cellar, lamented the sad state of

Nimitz Hotel, 340 East Main Street. *Author's photograph.*

current drinking affairs. "Such happens in the course of time," he wrote, "that the place which once furnished the liquid that added to the merriment of the merrymakers now furnishes pure drinking water—not even a blind tiger [a place that sells illegal booze] is maintained in the place that others might think splendidly fit for such purposes."

The bar at the Nimitz continued to operate after the brewery closed. Townspeople, stage drivers, salesmen, travelers, soldiers and politicians gathered there to drink, gossip and socialize.

William Sydney Porter, better known as the writer O. Henry, spent time at the Nimitz in the 1880s. He came to town to collect subscriptions for his San Antonio newspaper, the *Rolling Stone*. Mrs. Dora Reagan, granddaughter of Charles Nimitz, recalled hearing her grandfather tell of O. Henry spending several days at the hotel, mostly at the bar, soaking up the local culture. Inspired by that visit, O. Henry wrote one of his best-known short stories, "A Chaparral Prince."

The Germans had a lukewarm relationship with O. Henry. They admired his talent but weren't always charmed with his treatment of their culture. An article in the *Fredericksburg Standard* concluded, "The beautiful story of 'The Chaparral Prince' which uses as a setting the one time frequent mail robberies on the mail routes from here to San Antonio and which pretends to depict the life of the people of our country, was undoubtedly begun while the writer was at the hotel."

BANK SALOON

The corner of Main and Adams Streets in Fredericksburg, across from the Gillespie County Courthouse, is one of the busiest and most historic locations in the Texas Hill Country. John Hunter ran a saloon on that corner as early as 1850. Hunter also served as the Gillespie County Clerk, and he kept all the county records at the saloon, there being no courthouse at the time.

One night, a group of soldiers from Fort Martin Scott came into Hunter's Saloon. After a few too many drinks, one of the soldiers got into an argument with Hunter. Someone threw a punch, and a fight broke out. A few minutes later, the soldier lay dead on the barroom floor. He bled to death from a stab wound.

The next evening, a group of soldiers came into town to avenge the death of their friend. Unable to find John Hunter, who had advance warning and had found a hiding place in a house on Live Oak Creek, the soldiers burned his saloon. Not only the building but also all three books of the county records went up in flames.

Edward Maier bought the property in 1860. In 1874, he built a two-story rock building on the corner that still stands.

In the 1880s, Temple D. Smith, a banker from Virginia, rented the building to house the Bank of Fredericksburg. The colorful Judge A.O. Cooley had a law office on the second floor of the Maier Building.

Temple Smith completed his Bank of Fredericksburg building across the street (today Kowert Real Estate) in 1887. When Temple Smith moved out of the Maier Building, Richard Maier ran a saloon there. Locals called Maier's business the Bank Saloon. Maier ran it until Prohibition closed it in 1920.

Richard Maier's son Henry opened a grocery store in the building. Later, the building housed a Piggly Wiggly Food Store.

BRAEUTIGAM'S SALOON

John W. Braeutigam bought the old Fort Martin Scott property on the outskirts of Fredericksburg from the government in March 1870. He built a saloon and store near the road and started the first dancehall in the Hill Country, called Braeutigam's Garten, in the old officer's quarters.

On September 10, 1884, four bandits murdered John Braeutigam after he refused to hand over the money in the cash drawer at the saloon.

BUCKHORN SALOON

The decor of saloons often reflected local culture. Cow horns and buffalo hides decorated saloons on the plains. Moose horns dangled from the ceiling in saloons in Montana. In the Texas Hill Country, interior decorators found interesting ways to use deer horns.

Antlers covered the walls of the Buckhorn Saloon, one of the most popular watering holes in Fredericksburg. The Buckhorn occupied the lot at the corner of Main and Crockett Streets, where Security State Bank now stands.

Heinrich Ochs acquired the one-hundred-by-two-hundred-foot corner lot in 1868. Ochs—known around town as the "Schullehrer," the schoolteacher—lived a small log house on the lot that doubled as a schoolhouse. He also taught classes in the Vereins Kirche. From 1859 to 1869, Ochs served as Gillespie county clerk.

When Heinrich died, his will divided his property between his two sons, Herman and Henry. Herman received the corner lot at Main and Crockett. He opened a saloon there called the Buckhorn.

By the beginning of the twentieth century, the Buckhorn Saloon, now a fine two-story rock building, was dispensing bottled beer and keg beer for five cents a glass, along with wine, whiskey, liquor and cigars. Bartenders kept the beer on ice. There was a billiard table and a pool table in the back of the main room.

Hermann Ochs served as sheriff of Gillespie County from 1910 to 1918. He sold the saloon to Otto Meurer in order to devote himself full time to the office of sheriff.

Mr. and Mrs. Meurer moved into the building and ran the saloon until the Volstead Act closed it in 1919. In the 1920s, Mr. and Mrs. Henry Keyser used the building as the Main Hotel. The Stehling family opened the Plaza Hotel on the property in 1926. That busy street corner has been the home of Security State Bank since 1941.

BISMARCK SALOON

Louis Gerhard owned the Bismarck Saloon on Main Street in Fredericksburg. The saloon sold Pabst Milwaukee Blue Ribbon Beer on tap and by the bottle. Gerhard, the local Pabst distributor, also sold beer wholesale to other saloons. In additional to beer, the Bismarck Saloon sold soda water, mineral water and fine cigars.

Bismarck Saloon, 1907, Fredericksburg. *Left to right*: Charlie Goehmann, Charles Schmidt, Otto Lindig and Sheriff John Klaerner. *Gillespie County Historical Society*.

The Bismarck Saloon occupied a two-story building with a covered porch, a beer cellar in the basement and a wagon yard and horse camp out back.

FARMERS HOME SALOON

The Farmers Home Saloon, owned by Hubert Kott, sold whiskey, brandy, wine and cigars in addition to fresh keg and bottled beer.

THE WHITE ELEPHANT SALOON

Of all the names for saloons in nineteenth-century Texas, the most popular had to be the White Elephant. Other Texas towns that had White Elephant Saloons included Abilene, Austin, Brownsville, Brenham, Bryan, Denison, El Paso, Lampasas, Laredo, Mobeetie and Wichita Falls.

The White Elephant Saloon in San Antonio stood on the north side of the Main Plaza near San Fernando Church. At the White Elephant Saloon in Fort Worth, gunfighter Luke Short got crossways with Longhaired Jim Courtright. Short drew first and gave Courtright the longest funeral procession the city of Fort Worth had ever seen. That was the long and short of it.

The White Elephant Saloon at 242 East Main Street in Fredericksburg may have been the swankiest joint of any saloon in Texas that carried the name. The building itself is a thing of beauty. John Kleck built it in 1888.

The side walls are limestone blocks of various sizes, but the front wall has fancier carved stones. The building has not one but three sets of French doors in front and ornamental wrought iron railing along the top. Until 1938, a wooden gallery shaded the walkway in front of the building. Customers tied their horses to a hitching post along San Saba Street.

Inside the building, the long wooden bar occupied the space along the west wall. On the back wall hung a large mirror with open shelves to hold an assortment of beer, brandy and liquor glasses. A large ice chest at the back of the room kept the beer kegs cold. There was a cistern beneath the floor near the front of the building.

Carbide lights lit up the bar at night. Later, workers installed electric lights when Pfeil's power plant made electricity available.

White Elephant Saloon, 242 East Main Street. *Author's photograph.*

To put the finishing touch on the front of his fancy saloon, John Kleck hired two stonemasons, A.W. Petmecky and a man named Thompson, to carve or mold an elephant and attach it to the outside wall above the middle door.

That assignment wasn't easy. There were not many elephant images in the Texas Hill Country back then.

As luck would have it, a merry-go-around operated by a gentleman from Italy came to town for a short stay at Marketplatz. For a small fee, children could ride around in a circle on the backs of wooden animals from around the world. The animals included a lion, a tiger—and an elephant.

Petmecky and Thompson borrowed the wooden elephant and made an imprint of its body by pressing it into a large container of moist sand. Then they poured cement containing lime into the imprint to form the elephant we see today.

A sign at the top of the bracketed front porch displayed the name of the saloon with the owner's name just above the elephant.

Thirteen saloons lined Fredericksburg's Main Street in the 1880s. Competition for customers was fierce. To draw in customers, the White

Elephant offered a variety of liquid refreshments, including quarts of white lightning for fifteen cents each.

In 1893, John Kleck leased the building to saloonkeepers John Klaerner and Henry Langerhans for twenty-five dollars a month, with an interesting provision in the lease that allowed Kleck to terminate the agreement if the railroad came to town.

The saloon, as it turned out, was a goldmine. Klaerner and Langerhans bought the contents for $1,400: $400 cash and a $1,000 loan. They paid off the loan in less than a year.

Frank Schaper had the misfortune of being the owner of the White Elephant when the legislature enacted Sunday Laws, making it unlawful for a saloon to open on the Sabbath. The owner, a strict law-abiding citizen, kept the front doors locked tighter than a bank vault every Sunday, but the back door had a faulty latch.

The rest of the week, the front doors opened in the early morning and closed around midnight. The back door, however, might stay open well past midnight if a hot poker game was in progress or business was especially good. That darned latch again.

Joe and George Klein bought the business from Frank Schaper in 1908. The Kleins rented the corner of the building to a barber.

The White Elephant Saloon served the men of Fredericksburg with distinction until 1920. Then Prohibition hit the booze industry like a herd of elephants.

Over the next fifty years, the building housed a tractor and farm implement company, a grocery store, a barbershop and a dealership for Hudson-Essex automobiles.

The origin of the name White Elephant comes from Southeast Asian culture. White elephants were sacred in that part of the world. They were pampered and did no work of any kind. By the time the term arrived in America, it had come to mean, sometimes in a tongue-in-cheek sort of way, an expensive but worthless investment.

The name White Elephant may also relate to the phrase "seeing the elephant"—a nineteenth-century expression that referred to a great adventure.

Some sources in Fredericksburg say the name came from a custom in parts of Germany of using a white elephant as a symbol for an eating and drinking establishment.

The name also had racial overtones on the segregated frontier. Black Elephant Saloons in Fort Worth, Brenham, Austin, Houston and San Antonio catered to Black Americans.

RUDOLPH ITZ SALOON

The Itz family built this two-story symmetrical structure, located at 320 West Main Street, shortly after the Civil War. The walls are made of limestone rubble covered in stucco. In its history, the building has been a store, hotel, saloon, meeting hall and residence.

In 1896, the building housed the McDougall's Hotel. A saloon, probably run by William McDougall, occupied the large front room on the first floor. The smaller rooms behind served as a keg room, a dining room, a kitchen and a bedroom. In 1899, the building housed "Herman's Saloon—A Popular Men's Resort."

In 1902, the Rudolph Itz Saloon, a popular watering hole for local drinkers, occupied the first floor. Hilmer Weber bought the saloon in 1913 and ran it for seven years until Prohibition shut it down. During Prohibition, the building housed a meat market. Today it is the Itz Inn B&B.

Itz Inn (old Rudolph Itz Saloon), 349 West Main Street. *Author's photograph.*

CAPITAL SALOON

The Schmidt brothers, proprietors of the Capital Saloon on Main Street, guaranteed "polite and courteous treatment" to all customers. The saloon served fine liquor, wine and ice cold Pabst by the glass or in the bottle. The bar offered a variety of mixed drinks. An interesting advertisement in the September 28, 1907 issue of the *Fredericksburg Standard* noted that "mail orders receive careful attention."

PETER'S

In 1903, Ed Peter and Herman Mosel opened a saloon and restaurant in a stone building on the corner of Main and Orange Streets in Fredericksburg. One year later, Peter bought out Mosel and became sole proprietor.

Carpenters built the large wooden hall behind the saloon in 1910. A breezeway connected the two buildings. Peter's Hall, with its large open floor space, was a dancehall and more. It was an all-purpose community center that served a multitude of functions.

The hall hosted community-wide events, including movies, dances, Sängerfests (singing contests), concerts and plays. Fredericksburg High School and St. Mary's High School held their graduations there. For a time, Fredericksburg High School played basketball at Peter's Hall.

Anticipating Prohibition, Ed Peter bought a soda fountain from Hanisch and Payne Drug Store in Fredericksburg. Throughout the 1920s and early '30s, Peter's sold short-order food, fountain drinks, candy and near beer.

The heyday of Peter's Hall was the time before television. People spent leisure hours with friends and neighbors—eating, drinking, dancing, singing and socializing.

Then in the 1950s, business at Peter's declined. Television had changed entertainment habits and social patterns. People stayed home more—watching *I Love Lucy* and eating TV dinners. Peter's Hall was from another time, and its time had passed.

By 1960, the old wooden building needed repair, but the owners decided to sell the property, which sat on prime Main Street real estate, rather than repair the hall and keep the business going.

Workers razed Peter's in 1960 to make way for the Community Savings and Loan building—now Fredericksburg BBVA Bank.

THE LAST BASTION OF THE FRONTIER

Prohibition turned down the volume along Fredericksburg's Main Street. Muffled sounds behind locked doors and drawn curtains replaced laughter and merriment on Saturday night.

Prohibitionists praised the new law they hoped would heal an American society beset with alcoholism, crime and family violence, although some historians insist that Prohibition was as much about politics as drinking. Prohibition, they say, was in part about the desire of the wealthy class to suppress the working man's vote by shutting down the places where political ideas formed and unions organized.

Fredericksburg had no unions, and voters (men only until 1919) cared little for the politics of Prohibition. They just wanted beer.

On May 24, 1919, Gillespie County voted against Prohibition by a 10 to 1 margin (140 for Prohibition and 1,491 against). That same day, voters soundly rejected women's suffrage by an even bigger margin (135 for and 1,562 against).

The *Fredericksburg Standard* left no doubt where it stood on Prohibition. In November 1919, editor Robert Penniger wrote, "A ranger killed in ferreting out bootleg whiskey. 10,000 bootleggers now in Texas. The state papers, in favor of prohibition, report this. Verily, prohibition proves to be a blessing of satan."

Prohibition turned out to be a draconian and largely unenforceable law that proved especially cruel for German Americans. At times, the temperance movement appeared to be aimed directly at the Germans, whose love of beer was no secret. Some Prohibition advocates even used racist rhetoric to connect German Americans, beer and support for the enemy during World War I.

John Strange, Prohibition advocate and lieutenant governor of Wisconsin, spoke for a lot of people when he said, "We have German enemies across the water. We have German enemies in this country too. And the worst of all our German enemies, the most treacherous, the most menacing, are Pabst, Schlitz, Blatz and Miller."

Whatever the intentions, the movement to outlaw alcohol seemed to dovetail with the anti-German attitude that ran strong in the country. There is little doubt that anti-German feelings caused by the war made Prohibition easier to pass.

When some sanity prevailed and the country repealed Prohibition in 1933, most people assumed old-time saloons would return, but saloons never made a comeback. They had roots in an earlier time.

Fredericksburg Brewing Company, 245 East Main Street. *Author's photograph.*

The state legislature in Austin, still run by prohibitionists, did everything possible to kill saloons for good. For the next forty years, it was illegal in Texas to sell whiskey by the drink.

And so saloons marked the beginning and the end of an era. They represented the first imprint and the last bastion of the Texas frontier culture.

After Prohibition, drinking establishments in Fredericksburg slowly became more inclusive and more polite. They became bars, pubs, taverns, lounges, cantinas, breweries, beer gardens, icehouses and tasting rooms.

Unlike saloons, the commercial brewing business did return, although in some cases on a smaller scale. Today, in an ironic twist with some poetic justice thrown in, the big breweries are struggling (some have shut down), while business is hopping at several local breweries in Fredericksburg and dozens more across the Hill Country.

BEER AND AMMO

Hill Country people looked for new places to drink and new ways to socialize after the end of Prohibition. In Fredericksburg and South Texas, icehouses became unlikely drinking establishments and social centers until beer gardens came back in style.

In the beginning, Texas icehouses actually sold ice—specifically, twenty-five-pound blocks of ice to use in home iceboxes in the days before refrigeration. In fact, icehouses sold nothing but ice until a farsighted owner saw a way to expand his business. He took advantage of the cold temperatures in the ice vault to store and sell not only ice but also beer and all kinds of food items that needed to be kept cold. Other icehouses quickly copied the idea.

In South Texas, where cold beer was a big seller, owners brought in chairs and set up domino and pinochle tables to take advantage of the cool air from the ice vault. People in the neighborhood would stop by after work to have a beer, tell a joke, play some dominoes and catch up on the local gossip. On weekends, they brought the whole family and made an evening of it.

Icehouses flourished even after most homes got electric refrigerators and air-conditioning. They adapted to particular situations. In towns near lakes and rivers, icehouses sold bait, tackle and fishing licenses. In the Hill Country, where deer hunting is a major industry, icehouses sold ammo, and they added cold storage units so hunters could store their dressed deer carcasses.

While there is some dispute over what constitutes an honest-to-goodness Texas icehouse, many experts agree that the icehouse/beer joint/community center concept first formed in post-Prohibition San Antonio—a place with few taboos against beer drinking and where an ice cold foamy beverage brought some comfort from the heat on a sultry summer evening. By the late 1940s, just about every San Antonio neighborhood had one.

Icehouses were not fancy, and no two were alike. Built mostly of cinder block or metal, they were boxy, functional and architecturally unattractive. There was not a lot of information on the outside of the building to identify the place. Pickup trucks parked in a crooked line on the dirt or gravel parking lot. Some icehouse parking lots looked like they were paved with beer bottle caps.

Inside, decor favored the plain and simple, with bare concrete floors and mismatched tables and chairs. Some icehouses had pool tables, jukeboxes and TV sets to watch the game of the week. A few neon beer signs adorned the walls. Several Fredericksburg icehouses sponsored teams in the local bowling and softball league and proudly displayed their dusty trophies behind the counter.

However, all real icehouses had two things in common: ice cold beer (often advertised as "the coldest beer in town") and a friendly atmosphere for the whole family. While some icehouses sold liquor, they served no mixed drinks (liquor by the drink was illegal in Texas until 1970), although in Fredericksburg, no one objected if one of the regulars brought in a bottle of schnapps to share on a cold winter afternoon.

An evening at an icehouse was just plain fun. Adults drank beer, played pinochle, gossiped and socialized. Children played baseball, kick the can and freeze tag in the open space out back.

Icehouses once played an important role in the community life of Fredericksburg. Once upon a time, every major road leading into town had an icehouse.

It is interesting that while South Texas icehouses evolved into neighborhood taverns, icehouses in Central, North and East Texas, the more religiously conservative part of the state, became convenience stores. At first, owners sold eggs, butter, milk and soft drinks in addition to ice. Then, as business picked up, proprietors brought in metal shelves and racks and added bread, snacks, chewing tobacco and cigarettes to the inventory.

The most famous icehouse/convenience store of them all began in 1927 when John Jefferson Green, an employee of the Southland Ice Company of Dallas, began selling eggs, milk and bread from the dock of the icehouse where he worked. The business became 7-Eleven Inc.

STEIN'S ICE FACTORY

A market for ice emerged in the early twentieth century when families in Fredericksburg began buying iceboxes for the kitchen to keep perishable foods cold. In 1907, Franz Stein, born in Germany, started Stein's Ice Factory to supply refrigerators with block ice. In 1913, he built a new ice factory in the 200 block of West Schubert Street in Fredericksburg. An eighty-horsepower steam boiler generated the power to make the ice. Customers could pick up their own ice at the factory, or the factory would deliver ice to their homes for a small fee.

Oscar Stein took over the ice factory when his father retired. Later, Oscar sold the business to dairymen Alonzo and Johnny Evers (cousins to Admiral

Chester Nimitz), who operated it until it closed in the 1960s. The building was later torn down.

Stein's Ice Factory never evolved into a community tavern or convenience store, but it did branch out into other businesses. Early on, Stein's added cold storage facilities for hunters to store deer and turkeys. Since Stein's already had ice, it was a natural step to make and sell ice cream. Alonzo Evers sold milk from his dairy at the icehouse.

WILLIE'S IZE BOX

Felix and Eddie Willie opened the first real icehouse in Fredericksburg in 1948. Willie's Ize Box occupied a lot on the edge of town at 907 East Main Street in South Heights (between what is today Cowgirl Kim's and Fredericksburg Escapes—across from Dairy Queen).

Over the years, the Willie brothers made several additions to the building to accommodate the growing business. Those additions included an air-conditioned customer lounge and a cold storage vault for hunters to store their deer and turkeys.

The Deluxe Ize Box (formerly Willie's Ize Box), 907 East Main Street. *Gillespie County Historical Society.*

Willie's Ize Box sold fresh meats, dried sausage, staple groceries, full and factory-marked ice, beer, whiskey, sporting goods, magazines, ammunition and bait. Sportsmen could buy hunting and fishing licenses at Willie's Ize Box. As a special treat, customers could buy head cheese, Blutwurst (blood sausage) and Leberwurst (liver sausage) every Friday.

Willie's had a crowd of regulars who drank beer there, especially after work and on weekends. In addition to the locals, a steady stream of Ausländers stopped by, especially during deer season. Customers could have a cold one in Willie's lounge or buy "beer to go—cold or warm—by the case, six pack or bottle."

When Felix Willie's health declined, he sold his interest in the business to his brother Eddie in 1971. Felix died later that year. The Willie family sold the business in 1974.

Willie's Ize Box became the Deluxe Ice House until it closed in the late 1970s.

JIM'S ICE HOUSE

One of the best-known icehouses in Fredericksburg was Jim's—located at 528 West Main Street on the west side of town (today Bigs Convenience Store at the corner of Main and Bowie Streets). James Turrentine, a navy World War II veteran, built the cinder tile building with a flat roof in 1953.

While Willie's Ize Box catered to hunters, Jim's Ice House was more of a neighborhood convenience store, beer joint and gathering place. Jim's had an air-conditioned customer lounge and a barbecue pit out back. Customers could buy beer (by the bottle, six pack or case), cold drinks, liquor, groceries, block and crushed ice and picnic supplies.

Later, the building that housed Jim's Ice House expanded, and the Tower Restaurant moved in. The Tower became one of the most popular restaurants in town, especially for the younger crowd. Jim's customers could order a burger or finger steaks from the Tower and wash it down with an ice cold Lone Star longneck from Jim's.

In the 1960s, James Turrentine sold Jim's Ice House and bought Fair Park Service Station and Grocery at 512 South Adams in Fredericksburg (corner of South Adams and Walch—where Neffendorf and Blocker, PC is today). Ed Straube built Fair Park Service Station and Grocery around 1950. Straube had made a name for himself cooking and selling Sunday barbecue.

Jim's Ice House, 528 West Main Street. *Gillespie County Historical Society.*

Fair Park Service Station and Grocery evolved into an expanded version of an icehouse that sold gasoline, barbecue and chili in addition to the regular icehouse fare. The store housed a bar, a seating area, a television and a jukebox.

The business closed in the late 1970s.

87 ICE BOX

The 87 Ice Box still stands on the corner of Highway Street and US Highway 87 South, although it doesn't get a lot of attention these days. Just a lonely building at a busy intersection.

But there was a time when 87 Ice Box was a popular community gathering place. Of course, that was back in the day when people actually knew their neighbors. Today, too many people spend time staring at a computer screen or taking political cheap shots at one another on Facebook.

Milton and Carleen Grobe owned the 87 Ice Box. Carleen told me,

> *Milton and I opened 87 Ice Box on November 1, 1961. We sold beer and soft drinks, but 87 was also a convenience store. We sold bread, milk, eggs and canned goods. We sold ice cream. We even sold steaks, hamburger meat and cold cuts. We had a meat slicer for salami and baloney.*

87 Ice Box, 700 South Washington Street. *Author's photograph.*

A fisherman on his way to his favorite hole on the Pedernales could buy fishing tackle at 87 Ice Box. Customers could buy fireworks for Christmas and the Fourth of July.

Once inside, customers usually found a reason to hang around awhile. There was never a shortage of cold beer, bad jokes and animated conversation. The 87 Ice Box had a pinball machine, a jukebox and a pool table. Carleen Grobe recalled,

> *The best part of the business was the customers. Our regular customers were our friends and neighbors. We were like family. We went fishing together. Our children went to school together. We would meet at 87 Ice Box on weekends and on special occasions. The adults talked and drank beer inside while the kids played in the open space out back. We knew they were safe back there. If we had been fishing, we had a fish fry. We spent many evenings laughing together and having fun.*
>
> *Milton and I worked long hours, but we loved it. I spent a big part of my life there. I have a lot of good memories of that place.*

LAKEWAY ICE HOUSE

Lakeway Ice House on the North Llano Highway had an air-conditioned customer lounge. Owners Mr. and Mrs. Dean Sanders and Mr. and Mrs.

Willie Filter sold ice, beer, cold drinks, groceries, smoked sausage and jerky. The owners built a cold storage unit so hunters could store deer and turkeys.

SUNSET VILLAGE ICE HOUSE

Jack Lawrence built Sunset Village Ice House at 186 North Milam Street in Fredericksburg. Sunset Village sold ice, cold drinks, beer, cold cuts, cheese and some groceries. Outdoorsmen could buy hunting and fishing supplies. Mr. and Mrs. Richard Beckmann bought Sunset Village in 1970. Today, the business is called Sunset Village Drive-In Grocery.

Fredericksburg icehouses, like German beer halls, were family gathering places. They served an important social function in Fredericksburg from the end of World War II until the 1970s, when anti-German feelings in Texas faded and beer gardens came back into fashion. By the 1990s, the real Fredericksburg icehouses had closed.

PUT A CORK IN IT

The Gillespie County wine industry is a twenty-first century financial juggernaut, but fifty years ago, no one could have predicted the level of success it would achieve. Back then, it was more of a hobby than a business. Gillespie County wine, like beer, had homely beginnings, got crushed by Prohibition and then made a dazzling comeback in the second half of the twentieth century.

The German immigrants brought wine-making skills with them to Texas in the 1840s. They preferred beer but had enjoyed wine since the Romans introduced them to it centuries earlier.

Before World War I, the Hill Country Germans made wine at home. They used wild mustang grapes and mountain grapes, but they also imported vines to grow different varieties of grapes.

In the 1880s, John Meusebach had a small vineyard at his nursery in Loyal Valley. He grew fourteen varieties of grapes from all over the world. A good argument can be made that the roots of the Hill Country wine industry sprouted in Meusebach's Loyal Valley nursery.

A lot of German families had small orchards, and quite a few probably cultivated grapevines. Carl Leyendecker and his family lived in the 100 block of East Austin Street in Fredericksburg. Before World War I, Leyendecker had a vineyard on the eastern end of the block in the direction of the Llano Road. The family made wine for sale. They stored hundreds of gallons of wine in their huge cellar.

But the boys in town stole so many of Leyendecker's grapes that he moved his vineyard to a ten-acre site northeast of Fredericksburg.

Beginning in the early twentieth century, and probably earlier, the Gillespie County Fair showcased local wines. Competition categories included white, red, mustang grape and mountain grape.

Texas was something of a viticultural frontier at the turn of the twentieth century. There may have been twenty vineyards across the state. Prohibition put almost all of them out of business.

While crushing grapes and making wine on a large scale may seem relatively new to the Hill Country, the roots of the commercial wine industry in Gillespie County date to at least the early twentieth century. One of the oldest wineries in Texas began outside Fredericksburg just before World War I.

Ludwig Vorauer brought his talents as a winemaker and nurseryman from Reid, Austria, to Gillespie County in 1913. He and his wife, Lina, settled on a small place three miles east of Fredericksburg, about a mile off Cave Creek Road.

Ludwig first tried cotton farming, but the bottom fell out of the cotton market at the start of World War I. He did a little better raising peanuts. He and some of his neighbors shipped what some say was the first train carload of peanuts from Gillespie County.

A nurseryman at heart, Vorauer spent every spare moment piddling in his nursery and his vineyard. He raised pecan trees, various kinds of fruit trees, shade trees, evergreens, palms, weeping willows, flowering shrubs and hedge plants. He planted his first grape vines in 1913.

Ludwig Vorauer, as it turned out, had a green thumb all the way up to the elbow. He soon quit farming, devoting all of his time and energy to his nursery and vineyard.

Prohibition put a cork in the American wine industry from 1920 to 1933, even though few citizens in these parts supported the law. (Local legend says "The cow's in the corn" was the Gillespie County Sheriff's Office's code that tipped off local citizens when federal agents came poking around the neighborhood.)

Ludwig Vorauer's winery, called the Texas Winery, jumped back into business after the repeal of Prohibition in 1933. His wines, advertised as the "Pride of Fredericksburg," included burgundy, sherry and blackberry. He also made sauterne (a sweet white wine) and tokay (another sweet white wine) named for the Tokaj (pronounced Tokā) region of Hungary.

Pride of Fredericksburg: Dark Red Wine, the Texas Winery. *Author's photograph.*

The Vorauer family worked hard at the winery, especially at harvest time. Father, mother and children picked grapes all day, took a quick break for dinner and crushed the grapes at night. Before electricity came in 1940, the crusher had to be cranked by hand. It was no job for a lightweight.

By 1937, Vorauer's Texas Winery was one of five registered wineries in the state. At the time, Texas Winery may have been the largest vineyard and winery combination in Texas.

Ludwig Vorauer shipped wine all over Texas and to other states, except where prohibited by law. Local business that sold Pride of Fredericksburg Wine included City Café, Palace Package Store, Sunnyside Hut, Kallenberg's Pharmacy, Sunnyside Liquor Store, Sunnyside Tavern, Peter's Bar, Richard Schmidtzensky's, Hotel Nimitz and Security Café.

Then, in October 1937, Ludwig Vorauer fell off the bumper of his truck while repairing his private telephone line. He died from his injuries a few days later.

When Ludwig died, his wife, Lina, son Carl, daughter Freida and son Max ran the business until it closed in 1956.

Although not fully appreciated in his lifetime, Ludwig Vorauer was a visionary. His winery established Gillespie and surrounding counties as wine country. When discussing the future of the Hill Country wine business back in 1964, Victor Nixon and his father-in-law B.L. Enderle reminded a *Harper Herald* reporter that the groundwork for a future industry had already been done.

Old barrel house, the Texas Winery, Fredericksburg. *Author's photograph.*

"Ludwig Vorauer and son Carl at one time had a big vineyard and winery out on the Burnet Road," Nixon recalled, "and they were quite successful at growing a variety of grapes."

A SLEEPING GIANT

A German named Halbedhl, while wandering across Texas, spotted a grapevine struggling to grow in poor, rocky soil. Franciscan Friars planted the vine in the eighteenth century. The friars came to Texas carrying rootstock of criolla (Spanish) grapes in their haversacks.

Impressed with the plant's will to survive, Halbedhl took a cutting from that sacred vine and replanted it on a picturesque hillside overlooking the Pedernales River near Fredericksburg. As he placed the plant in the ground and carefully shoveled dirt around it with his hands, Halbedhl could hear the blessings of the friars off in the distance.

The Hill Country wine industry began on that hillside over 150 years ago, biding its time until it roared to life in the late twentieth century.

Great story, but none of it is true. Haldedhl is a myth, and his adventure is a convenient fairytale made up to sell wine.

Once upon a time, the Hill Country wine industry existed only in the minds of romantics and visionaries. A handful of zealots worked behind the scenes, doing the necessary experiments and tedious grassroots calculations, but the rest of the world paid little attention.

In 1971, Rae Hennon began quietly experimenting with different varieties of grapes at his place on Knopp School Road northeast of Fredericksburg. Hennon grew a variety of grapes and painstakingly recorded the characteristics of each variety as to size, color, taste, weight, hardiness to cold temperatures and disease resistance.

Today, Rae Hennon is all but forgotten, but his fingerprints are all over the Hill County wine industry. Retired Gillespie County extension agent Durey Menzies called Hennon "one of the unsung heroes of the Gillespie County wine business."

There were at least two other experimental vineyards in Gillespie County in the early 1970s: one at the Dr. E.A. Blackburn place near the Pecan Creek Community northwest of Fredericksburg and the other at the Rodman Saville place near Tivydale.

At the time, there was one registered winery in Texas—the Val Verde Winery in Del Rio (started in 1882—it survived making church wine). Prohibition killed the rest. A couple of farms near Hondo produced grapes for experimental purposes, and some Texas Tech University professors had been experimenting with grapes and wine on the South Plains near Lubbock since 1968. With those exceptions, the Texas wine industry barely existed.

Real Texans drank beer—on tap, in the can or in the longneck bottle. Sissies drank wine. Ask a typical Texan in 1970 to suggest a red and a white wine, and chances are he would recommend Ripple (red) and Thunderbird (white), available at 7-Eleven stores for eighty-nine cents a bottle.

Established drinking habits, however, had started to change, even in Texas. With health- and weight-conscious Americans beginning to turn away from regular beer (light beer sales took off in the mid-'70s), and wine consumption predicted to double in the 1980s, people with deep pockets were betting significant amounts of money that Texas grapes and Texas wine were about to become big business.

If those predictions came true, an entrepreneur who got in early could make a fortune. It was the kind of wildcat atmosphere that attracted legitimate businessmen, mavericks, adventurers and some smooth operators looking to make a fast buck.

In the spring of 1974, when the Hill Country wine rumors had not yet risen above a whisper, a thirty-one-year-old marketing whiz, songwriter and fledgling winemaker named Dean Joyner attracted statewide attention when he and his wife, Barbara, leased the old Morris Ranch Schoolhouse

Morris Ranch Schoolhouse, Morris Ranch Road. *Author's photograph.*

from Fredericksburg Independent School District. In an ambitious project allegedly backed by the largest grape co-op in California, Joyner, with great fanfare and a ton of publicity, announced plans to plant a vineyard near the schoolhouse, on the side of a rocky hill, not far from the Pedernales River. He named his business Haversack Winery.

Joyner described his marketing strategy as the "back door approach." He would first market California wine in Texas, build up a cash flow and then "work back" to cultivating Texas grapes for a Texas wine.

The label on Haversack Wine read "from historic Fredericksburg, Texas," but it was pure California, born, bred and bottled. (To be honest, it did spend a little time in a Fredericksburg warehouse.) Joyner also claimed that each bottle contained 5 percent "mission wine," made from criolla grapes, brought to Texas and California in the eighteenth century by friars in their haversacks.

Dean Joyner told a good story. He also had connections, and he knew how to make a splash. The elaborate ceremony that coincided with the planting of the first grapevines at Haversack Winery could have been scripted by a Hollywood screenwriter.

A curious crowd gathered at four o'clock in the afternoon on March 1, 1975, at the Morris Ranch School. Guich Koock, film and TV actor and one of the owners of Luckenbach, served as master of ceremonies. A vocal group called Die Fröhliche Vier (the Happy Four) sang "The Haversack Ballad" (an original composition written by Dean Joyner). Reverend Dean Pratt, pastor of St. Barnabas Episcopal Church in Fredericksburg, read the Bible story describing Jesus's first miracle—changing water into wine at the wedding in Cana. That marvel was the first, but not the last, of the biblical metaphors invoked that day.

The crowd then heard the story of the Spanish priests bringing grapevines to Texas in their haversacks—a dubious claim that gave the winery its name. Mrs. Werner Knopp read the haversack legend in German. Dean Joyner read it in English. Dr. Joe B. Franz, well-known author and director of the Texas State Historical Association, spoke about the history of grapes and wine in Texas.

Then, right on cue, the bells at the Morris Ranch Schoolhouse tolled, signaling the arrival of Franciscan friars from Mission San Jose in San Antonio. The friars spoke about the importance of Texas vineyards and Texas wine, used in Holy Communion, in the early Spanish missions. As the friars conducted the centuries-old "blessing of the grapes" ceremony, Lady Bird Johnson stepped forward and planted the first grapevine.

According to reports, Mrs. Johnson enjoyed an occasional glass of a Haversack wine called Straw Blanc. "She's been serving this wine out at the ranch," Joyner told a *San Antonio Express* reporter. "I've shipped wine to Lynda [Rabb], and she's given it away all over New England. They're really promoting the wine for me."

Mrs. Johnson's participation in the opening ceremony gave Haversack Winery some as yet undeserved credibility. Many major newspapers in Texas carried the story of Haversack Winery, often as a feature in the Sunday edition.

As for Dean Joyner, just about everyone agreed that he was a likeable guy, and he seemed on the level. He certainly brought a lot of attention to Fredericksburg. Whatever he did made news, even scripting a self-serving fairytale about haversacks, a wandering German, sprouting grapevines and friars chanting off in the distance.

That fall, Haversack Winery hosted the very first wine festival in Texas. Attendees drank Haversack Wine and nibbled on a 2,100-pound chunk of cheddar cheese. Pehl's Old Time Band from Fredericksburg played German tunes. The Ballet Folklorico España of San Antonio performed Mexican folk dances. Vendors sold Haversack Wine T-shirts. Volunteers demonstrated an old wine press, and youngsters stomped grapes.

Adults paid five dollars to get in, but the price of admission included a special Haversack Wine glass and the wine to fill it—over and over again. Only when supplies ran low did the party show signs of slowing down.

That evening, some of the guests who'd had way too much to drink tried to suck wine from the wine press. When the sun came up the next morning, quite a few cars, covered with dew, still lined Morris Ranch Road.

Headaches and hangovers aside, the original Texas Wine Festival focused a lot of media attention on the Hill Country. The word spread. People all over Texas began to associate Fredericksburg with wine.

At first, the clamor and celebration drowned out the complaints. A lot of people ordered Haversack Wine by mail, but the orders never arrived. When a reporter for the *San Antonio Express* called the Haversack office in Fredericksburg to investigate, he got a recorded message saying the phone was "no longer in service." Unable to reach anyone at the office for weeks, the *San Antonio Express* Action Line column on May 10, 1976, reported that the Haversack Wine Company was "out of business."

"Not so," said Dean Joyner, when finally spotted by reporters. He had a simple explanation. His home in Fredericksburg sold, so he moved into quarters at Morris Ranch Schoolhouse. He had trouble getting a phone connection. (It took four months.) And all the mail-order wine would be shipped just as soon as the company solved a few minor logistical problems. The *San Antonio Express* printed a retraction.

But Haversack had bigger problems than logistics and phone lines. The "backdoor approach" didn't generate enough income to cover expenses.

The company had run out of money months ago, and now it ran out of credit. It existed for a time on flashy headlines, big talk and loud promises. Then time ran out.

In June 1976, Stein Lumber Company of Fredericksburg sued Dean Joyner for a stack of unpaid bills. In July, a Houston design and graphics company sued Joyner for unpaid invoices. In December 1976, the Fredericksburg School Board began the process of cancelling the lease agreement with the Haversack Winery. The company had, as Superintendent Crandall Young explained, "defaulted on its lease payments."

Pontotoc Weingarten, 320 West Main Street. *Author's photograph.*

By the spring of 1977, Dean Joyner and Gillespie County had parted ways. Weeds grew on the rocky hillside that once attracted so much attention, hope, comedy and drama. The most ambitious wine project in Texas history had fizzled.

After a time of denial, then shock and finally acceptance, Fredericksburg and Gillespie County chalked up the incident to a learning experience, took a deep breath and moved on. Oh well! At least everybody had some fun. And in a strange way, the shenanigans at Haversack Winery, and all the publicity (good and bad) they created, put a spotlight on Gillespie County and may have helped awaken a sleeping giant. The wine business, after all, is a romantic adventure. It attracts dreamers, poets, pirates and risk-takers.

Whatever Haversack's role in it, the wine industry in Gillespie County began to grow faster than the national debt. In 1976, Bob Oberhelmann planted three acres of grapes at his farm near Eckert. His Oberhelmann/Bell Mountain Winery, the first in the area, opened in 1983. Oberhelmann is also responsible for the Bell Mountain region's designation as an AVA (American Viticultural Area), the first designated wine area located entirely in the state of Texas. (Today, there are eight.)

In 1981, Karl and Judy Koch of Corpus Christi planted an acre of grapes at Pedernales Vineyards south of Fredericksburg on Highway 16. Grape Creek Vineyards, between Fredericksburg and Stonewall, the first of the Highway 290 vineyards, opened in 1983. Dr. Richard Becker and his wife, Bunny, of San Antonio established Becker Vineyards between Fredericksburg and Stonewall in 1992.

Right: Grape Creek Vineyards, Fredericksburg. *Author's photograph.*

Below: Grape Creek Vineyards, Fredericksburg. *Author's photograph.*

In 1970, Texas could claim one registered winery. In 2023, there are over five hundred wineries in the state. The Hill Country alone has over fifty wineries and counting.

Chapter 8

In Search of a Beer Garden

We should look for someone to eat and drink with before looking for something to eat and drink.
—Epicurus

Art Kowert, editor of the *Fredericksburg Standard*, often commented on Fredericksburg culture in his weekly column, Around the Square. Kowert didn't mince words. He missed the old days. He expressed frustration with the lack of German atmosphere in the eating and drinking establishments in the years after World War II.

In December 1952, Kowert referenced an article in that month's edition of the *Farmer-Stockman Magazine.* The article described Fredericksburg as a German town with an old beer garden, although the editor had to admit "darned if we know" where that beer garden is. At the time, Fredericksburg was still recovering from Prohibition and the wave of anti-German feeling following the war.

The situation wouldn't improve anytime soon. In 1968, Kowert again lamented the lack of dyed-in-the-wool German restaurants in Fredericksburg. There were, he said,

> *some eating places in the city that have good German food, but we still think there is something lacking in the way of real down-to-earth German atmosphere.*

> *We don't have a refined Biergarten around with good old German songs wafting through the air, and the feel of Gemütlichkeit that supposedly should permeate the entire community but which we find hard to come by these days.*

But better times were coming. The transformation began with a gradual shift in attitudes. As each year passed, the anti-German feelings faded. At the same time, the postwar generation of Texas Germans more openly embraced their heritage. Familiar symbols of the German culture reappeared.

In the early 1960s, the Gillespie County Fair Association built a beer garden at the County Fairgrounds. It seemed a small thing, but the impact exceeded expectations. The beer garden was a hit. Another early German festival, Night in Old Fredericksburg, featured a beer garden starting in 1964. Locals and visitors loved the music, the food, the dancing and the merriment at the beer gardens. An old German tradition came back to life.

German pride resurfaced in other ways. In 1960, Das Glockenspiel, an all-out German American restaurant, opened on Main Street. The opening of the Sunday House Restaurant in 1967 highlighted German architecture, German culture and German food. In 1970, Elgin and Betty Usener added the Bavarian-inspired façade to Betty's Restaurant (today Auslander). The Wild Game Dinner, first held in the early 1970s, raised a lot of money for worthy causes in Gillespie County but also carried on an old German tradition of serving wild game during celebrations.

In 1974, Bill Wareing bought and refurbished the old building on Main Street next to Dietz Bakery and turned it into an eatery called the Domino Parlor. The food at the Domino Parlor wasn't German, but the place had a central location and a lively beer garden where tourists and locals could eat and drink outside in a casual atmosphere. The Domino Parlor became one of the more popular restaurants in town. The beer garden had a lot to do with its popularity.

Two years later, Guich Koock bought and renovated the old Krauskopf Building on West Main Street and turned it into an eatery called Oma Koock's. Not only did Oma Koock's have a large airy beer garden, but German food also made up the main menu items.

It might not have been apparent at the time, but Das Glockenspiel, Betty's Restaurant, the Sunday House Restaurant, the Domino Parlor and Oma Koock's represented a turning point in the long and complicated history of German culture, food and drink in Fredericksburg. German food, never wildly popular with the general public, found a niche and achieved a level of

Altdorf Restaurant and Biergarten, 310 West Main Street. *Author's photograph.*

Der Lindenbaum Restaurant, 312 East Main Street. *Author's photograph.*

Pasta Bella Italian Restaurant, 103 South Llano Street. *Author's photograph.*

respect and acceptance. Beer gardens became fashionable again. German pride soared. After laying low for much of the twentieth century, German culture in Texas experienced a renaissance.

Today, visitors come to Fredericksburg for its festivals, fairs, museums, art galleries, scenery, shopping, food, wine, craft beer and German culture. Other people come here from all over the world to live and work, and they bring their culture with them.

As a result, the modern Fredericksburg food and drink culture is an exciting mixture of traditional, contemporary urban and international cuisines. The German food in Fredericksburg's cafés and restaurants is better than ever, but there are also American, Mexican, Cajun, French, Italian, Mediterranean, Asian, Caribbean and Southwestern offerings—everything from Schnitzel to sushi.

The rich history of food and drink in Fredericksburg is still being written in the restaurants, cafés, bistros, pubs, breweries and wine gardens along Main Street. There is a story in every bite and an adventure in every glass.

About the Author

Michael Barr is a writer and retired educator living an idyllic though modest life in Fredericksburg, Texas. (Teacher retirement only goes so far.) He likes to travel (he once spent a weekend in San Angelo), but his favorite place is the Texas Hill Country. His books include *Rope Burns and Lead Poisoning: The Wild West in Central Texas*, *Remembering Bulldog Turner*, *Cloyce Box: 6'4" and Bulletproof*, *A Hill Country Christmas: Hope for Hardscrabble Times* (contributor) and *Hill Country Hindsights: Stories from a Simpler Time*. Magazines that have printed his stories include *Southwestern Historical Quarterly*, *Old West Magazine*, *True West Magazine*, *Texas Highways Magazine* and *Rock and Vine Magazine*. His Hindsights column appears in the *Fredericksburg Standard*, the *Johnson City Record-Courier* and TexasEscapes.com on a semi-regular basis.

Lost Restaurants of Fredericksburg